Opera Journeys Libretto Series

GIOACHINO ROSSINI'S

La Cenerentola

COMPLETE LIBRETTO

Edited by Burton D. Fisher
Principal lecturer, *Opera Journeys Lecture Series*

Opera Journeys Publishing™/Boca Raton, Florida

WEB SITE: www.operajourneys.com   E MAIL: operaj@bellsouth.net

Libretto

La Cenerentola

La Cenerentola ('Cinderella'), translated from Italian, means "the one who sweeps the ashes or cinders (cenere) out of the fireplace." Similarly, in English, "Cinderella" literally means the "girl of the cinders."

ACT I

A shabby room in the home of Don Magnifico, Baron of Montefiascone.
There is a fireplace, a small table with a mirror and some chairs.

Clorinda, the Baron's older daughter, practices a chassè, a ballet step in which one leg virtually "chases" the other. Tisbe, the Baron's younger daughter, experiments with the placement of different flowers in her hair. Cinderella, the Baron's stepdaughter, blows the fire with a bellows in lieu of making coffee.

CLORINDA:
No, no, no: non v'è, non v'è chi trinciar sappia
così leggerissimo sciassé.

CLORINDA:
No one can perform a chassè as gracefully as I can.

Clorinda proceeds to perform the chassè, but very clumsily.

TISBE:
Sì, sì, sì: va bene lì. Meglio lì; no, meglio qui. Risaltar di più mi fa.

TISBE: *(placing flowers in her hair)*
Yes, it's better there. No, here it makes me stand out even more.

CLORINDA e TISBE:
A quest'arte, a tal beltà sdrucciolare ognun dovrà.

CLORINDA and TISBE:
Everyone will become spellbound by our beauty and class.

CENERENTOLA:
Una volta c'era un re, che a star solo s'annoiò:
cerca, cerca, ritrovò; ma il volean sposare in tre.

CINDERELLA: *(reciting a ditty)*
Once upon a time there was a king,
who became bored living without a wife.
He sought and found not one, but three suitable brides, all of whom wanted to marry him.

Cosa fa? Sprezza il fasto e la beltà. E alla fin scelse per sè l'innocenza e la bontà.
La la là. Li li lì. La la là.

And what did he do? He rejected good looks and ostentation, and in the end, chose an innocent and virtuous lady for his bride.

TISBE and CLORINDA:
Cenerentola, finiscila con la solita canzone.

TISBE and CLORINDA:
Cinderella, stop singing that same old ditty.

CENERENTOLA:
(Presso al fuoco in un cantone via lasciatemi cantar.)

CINDERELLA:
(I'll go into the corner near the fire so they won't hear me singing.)

Una volta c'era un re...

Once upon a time there was a king...

CLORINDA:
E due, e tre.

CLORINDA: *(dancing the chassè)*
And two, and three...

CLORINDA e TISBE:
La finisci sì o no? Se non taci ti darò!

CLORINDA and TISBE: *(threateningly)*
Will you stop it? Shut up or we'll beat the daylights out of you!

CENERENTOLA:
Una volta...

CINDERELLA: *(defying them)*
Once upon a time there was a king...

There is a knock at the door.

TUTTE:
Chi sarà?

ALL THREE:
Who can that be?

Alidoro, a philosopher and tutor of Prince Ramiro, appears, disguised as a beggar.

ALIDORO:
Un tantin di carità!

ALIDORO:
Please, a little charity!

CLORINDA e TISBE:
Accattoni! Via di qua!

CLORINDA and TISBE: *(disdainfully)*
Beggar! Get out of here!

CENERENTOLA:
Zitto, zitto: su prendete questo po' di colazione.

CINDERELLA:
Please! Quietly! Have this small breakfast!

Cinderella pours a cup of coffee and surreptitiously gives it to Alidoro, adding a piece of bread.

Ah non reggio alla passione, che crudel fatalità!

For Heaven's sake, hurry up! I can't bear this man's distress. How cruel his fate!

ALIDORO:
Forse il Ciel il guiderdone pria di notte vi darà.

ALIDORO:
Perhaps Heaven will reward your kindness before this day ends.

CLORINDA e TISBE:
Risvegliar dolce passione più di me nessuna sa.

CLORINDA and TISBE: *(strutting arrogantly)*
I am the only woman who knows how to arouse a man's ardent passion.

CLORINDA:
Ma che vedo! Ancora lì!

CLORINDA: *(turns and notices Alidoro)*
Now what do I see! You're still here!

TISBE:
Anche un pane? Anche il caffè?

TISBE:
And with bread? And even coffee?

CLORINDA e TISBE:
Prendi, prendi, questo a te!

CLORINDA and TISBE: *(hitting Cinderella)*
Take this! And this!

CENERENTOLA:
Ah! Soccorso chi mi dà?

CINDERELLA:
Help! Will someone help me?

ALIDORO:
Vi fermate, per pietà.

ALIDORO: *(vainly trying to interpose)*
For Heaven's sake, stop it!

There is loud knocking at the door. Cinderella opens the door, admitting the Prince's Courtiers.

CORTIGIANI:
O figlie amabil di Don Magnifico,
Ramiro il Principe - Or or verrà,
Al suo palagio vi condurrà.
Si canterà, si danzerà:
poi la bellissima fra l'altre femmine
sposa carissima per lui sarà.

COURTIERS:
Charming daughters of Don Magnifico, Prince Ramiro will soon arrive.
He will take you to his palace where there will be a ball, with singing and dancing.
At the ball, he will choose the most beautiful woman as his bride.

CLORINDA:
Ma dunque il Principe?

CORTIGIANI:
Or or verrà!

CLORINDA e TISBE:
E la bellissima?

CORTIGIANI:
Si sceglierà!

CLORINDA e TISBE:
Cenerentola vien qua. Le mie scarpe, il mio bonné. Cenerentola vien qua. Le mie penne, il mio collié. Nel cervello ho una fucina; son più bella e vo' trionfar. A un sorriso, a un'occhiatina Don Ramiro ha da cascar.

CENERENTOLA:
Cenerentola vien qua. Cenerentola va' là. Cenerentola va' su. Cenerentola vien giù. Questo è proprio uno strapazzo! Mi volete far crepar? Chi alla festa, chi al solazzo ed io resto qui a soffiar.

ALIDORO:
Nel cervello una fucina sta le pazze a martellar. Ma già pronta è la ruina. Voglio ridere a schiattar.

CORTIGIANI:
Già nel capo una fucina
sta le donne a martellar;
il cimento si avvicina
il gran punto di trionfar.

CLORINDA:
Date lor mezzo scudo. Grazie. Ai cenni del Principe noi siamo.

Clorinda notices that the beggar is still present.

Ancor qui siete? Qual tanfo! Andate, o ve ne pentirete!

CENERENTOLA:
Io poi quel mezzo scudo a voi l'avrei donato; ma non ho mezzo soldo. Il core in mezzo mi spaccherei per darlo a un infelice.

ALIDORO:
Forse al novello dì sarai felice.

CLORINDA:
But where is the prince?

COURTIERS:
He will be coming!

CLORINDA and TISBE:
How wonderful?

COURTIERS:
He will choose the most beautiful woman!

CLORINDA and TISBE:
Cinderella, bring my shoes, bonnet, feathers and necklace! I feel my head pounding. I am going to win the Prince because I am the most beautiful; I can smile seductively and attract him with a wink.

CINDERELLA:
Cinderella, come here! Go there! Go up! Come down!
What drudgery! Do you ladies want to kill me? Both of you go to the party and have a good time, while I must stay here and suffer.

ALIDORO:
A hammer pounds in the heads of those crazy girls. Nevertheless, I'm eager to burst into laughter when disaster befalls them.

COURTIERS:
Their heads are already pounding
and their hearts are throbbing.
There are many obstacles to overcome,
but in the end it will be a worthy triumph.

CLORINDA: *(handing a coin to Cinderella)*
Give them half a scudo! Thank you! We are at the Prince's service!

Are you still here? You smell! Leave, or you'll be sorry!

CINDERELLA: *(accompanying Alidoro)*
I would give you half a farthing, but I don't even have that to my name. I'd tear my heart in half to be able to help resolve your misfortune.

ALIDORO: *(emphatically, as he departs)*
Perhaps one day you will find happiness.

TISBE:
Cenerentola, presto. Prepara i nastri, i manti!

TISBE:
Cinderella, quickly, get the ribbons and cloaks!

CLORINDA:
Gli unguenti, le pomate.

CLORINDA:
Bring us our makeup articles!

TISBE:
I miei diamanti!

TISBE:
And my diamonds!

CENERENTOLA:
Uditemi, sorelle!

CINDERELLA:
Sisters, listen to me!

CLORINDA:
Che sorelle! Non profanarci con sì fatto nome.

CLORINDA: *(haughtily)*
What is this "sisters"! Don't humiliate us by calling us your sisters!

TISBE:
E guai per te se t'uscirà di bocca!

TISBE: *(threateningly)*
You'll regret it if you say that word again!

CENERENTOLA:
(Sempre nuove pazzie soffrir mi tocca.)

CINDERELLA: *(to herself)*
(Always suffering: the victim of their wickedness.)

TISBE:
Non v'è da perder tempo!

TISBE: *(approaching her sister)*
There's no time to lose!

CLORINDA:
Nostro padre avvisarne convien.

CLORINDA:
We must tell our father about the Prince.

Each one tries to prevent the other from entering their father's room.

TISBE:
Esser la prima voglio a darne tal nuova.

TISBE:
I want to be the first to give him the news.

CLORINDA:
Oh! Mi perdoni. Io sono la maggiore!

CLORINDA:
Excuse me, but I am the oldest!

TISBE:
No no, gliel vo' dir io!

TISBE: *(becoming enraged)*
No! I want to tell him!

CENERENTOLA:
È questo il dover mio. Io svegliare lo vuo. Venite appresso.

CINDERELLA:
This is my job. I'll go wake him up. Follow me!

TISBE:
Oh! Non la vincerai!

TISBE:
You're not going to get the upper hand!

CLORINDA:
Ecco egli stesso!

CLORINDA: *(observing from afar)*
There he's coming!

Don Magnifico enters, wearing a nightcap and robe. He is in an unfavorable mood. The daughters attempt to kiss his hand, but he refuses, withdrawing his hand from them. Then he addresses his daughters.

MAGNIFICO:
Miei rampolli femminini, vi ripudio; mi vergogno! Un magnifico mio sogno mi veniste a sconcertar.

MAGNIFICO:
My dear feminine pulchritude. I am repulsed and ashamed: you have interrupted a magnificent dream.

To himself, after noticing the girls giggling when he is not looking at them.

(Come son mortificate! Degne figlie d'un Barone!)

(How shameful the way these daughters of a Baron behave!)

Via; silenzio ed attenzione. State il sogno a meditar.

OK, girls, be quiet and pay attention. I want you to hear all about my dream!

Mi sognai fra il fosco e il chiaro un bellissimo somaro. Un somaro, ma solenne. Quando a un tratto, oh che portento!
Su le spalle a cento a cento gli spuntavano le penne ed in alto, *fsct*, volò!

I was half asleep, and half awake, dreaming about a most beautiful donkey. All of a sudden, a miracle occurred!
The donkey grew hundreds of feathers on its shoulders, and whoosh, it flew into the air!

Ed in cima a un campanile come in trono si fermò. Si sentiano per di sotto le campane sdindonar.

It landed atop a steeple, as if it was a throne. Below, one could hear the bells chiming and ringing: ding, dong.

Col cì, cì ciù ciù di botto mi faceste risvegliar. Ma d'un sogno sì intralciato. Ecco il simbolo spiegato.

Your endless chatter suddenly awakened me, but I think I can explain the meaning of my perplexing dream.

La campana suona a festa? Allegrezza in casa è questa.
Quelle penne? Siete voi.
Quel gran volo?
Plebe addio.
Resta l'asino di poi?

The bell that was pealing joyfully meant that there is happiness in my house!
The feathers? They were you, girls.
The flight? That meant that I shall rise in society and never have to deal with those crass, vulgar commoners again.

Ma quell'asino son io. Chi vi guarda vede chiaro che il somaro è il genitor.
Fertilissima Regina l'una e l'altra diverrà; ed il nonno una dozzina di nepoti abbraccierà.
Un Re piccolo di qua.
Un Re bambolo di là.
E la gloria mia sarà!

But I am that ass. One can immediately tell that your father is that beautiful ass.
One of you shall become a most fertile queen; and the grandfather will hug a dozen grandchildren. A little king will be over here, with everyone saying, "Your servant"; a baby king over there. The glory shall be mine!

CLORINDA:
Sappiate che fra poco!

CLORINDA: *(interrupting her father)*
Be prepared to receive that good news soon!

TISBE:
Il Principe Ramiro...

TISBE: *(interrupting)*
Prince Ramiro...

CLORINDA:
Che son tre dì che nella deliziosa...

CLORINDA:
He's been in his country estate for three days...

TISBE:
Vicino mezzo miglio venuto è ad abitar...

TISBE:
He's living nearby, about half a mile from here.

CLORINDA:
Sceglie una sposa...

CLORINDA:
He's going to be choosing a bride...

TISBE:
Ci mandò ad invitar.

TISBE:
He has invited us.

CLORINDA:
E fra momenti...

CLORINDA:
And any moment...

TISBE:
Arriverà per prenderci...

TISBE:
He will be arriving here to get us...

CLORINDA:
E la scelta la più bella sarà.

CLORINDA:
The most beautiful one will be chosen his bride.

MAGNIFICO:
Figlie, che dite!
Quel principon!

MAGNIFICO: *(in astonishment)*
Girls, what in the world are you saying!
A great Prince!

Quantunque io no'l conosco...
Sceglierà...
V'invitò...sposa...più bella!
Io cado in svenimento!

I don't know anything about him...
He will choose the fairest of you as his bride...
He invited you...wife...the most beautiful!
I feel quite faint!

Cenerentola, presto. Portami il mio caffè.

Cinderella, come quickly. Bring me coffee!

Cinderella quickly pours a cup of coffee and hands it to Don Magnifico.

Viscere mie.
Metà del mio palazzo è già crollata,
e l'altra è in agonia. Fatevi onore.
Mettiamoci un puntello.

Do your best, you fruits of my loin. I am broke;
half my palace is crumbling,
and the other half is slowly dying because it
lacks maintenance.

Pacing back and forth before his daughters.

Figlie state in cervello.
Parlate in punto e virgola.
Per carità: pensate ad abbigliarvi.
Si trata niente men che imprinciparvi.

Let's be wise!
Be careful what you say!
For Heaven's sake, think now about getting dressed:
it's a matter, no less, of becoming a Princess!

Magnifico and his daughters exit. Prince Ramiro enters, disguised as a squire.
He looks around the room cautiously.

RAMIRO:
Tutto è deserto. Amici? Nessun risponde. In
questa simulata sembianza le belle osserverò.
Né viene alcuno?

RAMIRO:
It's deserted. No one is here! No one answers.
In this squire's disguise, I'll be able to observe
the fair ladies. Is someone coming?

Eppur mi diè speranza il sapiente Alidoro, che
qui, saggia e vezzosa, degna di me trovar
saprò la sposa.

The wise Alidoro led me to believe that I would
find a virtuous and beautiful bride here: one
worthy of me.

Sposarsi...e non amar! Legge tiranna, che nel
fior de' miei giorni alla difficil scelta mi
condanna. Cerchiam, vediamo.

Getting married and not being in love? I am
condemned while still in the flower of my youth,
forced to marry to protect the royal lineage.

Cinderella enters, holding a tray with a cup and saucer.
She happily hums her ditty, Once upon a time there was a king."
She suddenly noticess Ramiro and drops the tray, which noisily clatters on the ground.

CENERENTOLA:
Ah! È fatta!

CINDERELLA:
Now I've done it!

RAMIRO:
Cos'è?

RAMIRO:
What is it?

CENERENTOLA:
(Che batticuore!)

CINDERELLA:
(My heart is pounding!)

RAMIRO:
Forse un mostro son io!

RAMIRO:
Perhaps you think I'm a monster!

CENERENTOLA:
Sì! No, signore!

CINDERELLA: *(nervously correcting herself)*
Yes! No, sir!

RAMIRO:
(Un soave non so che in quegl'occhi scintillo!)

RAMIRO:
(Something gentle sparkled in those eyes.)

CENERENTOLA:
(Io vorrei saper perché il mio cor mi palpitò?)

CINDERELLA:
(I wish I knew why my heart throbbed so much?)

RAMIRO:
(Le direi...ma non ardisco.)

RAMIRO:
(I would tell her, but I dare not.)

CENERENTOLA:
(Parlar voglio, e taccio intanto!)

CINDERELLA:
(I want to speak, but I'm speechless!)

CENERENTOLA e RAMIRO:
(Una grazia, un certo incanto par che brilli su quel viso!
Quanto caro è quel sorriso.
Scende all'alma e fa sperar.)

CENERENTOLA and RAMIRO:
(There is a certain grace about her;
an enchantment seems to shine in that face.
How loving his/her smile is; it seems to penetrate the soul and awaken hope.)

RAMIRO:
Del Baron le figlie io chiedo dove son?
Qui non le vedo.

RAMIRO: *(to Cinderella)*
I'm looking for the Baron's daughters.
Where are they? I don't see them here.

CENERENTOLA:
Stan di là nell'altre stanze.
Or verranno.

(Addio speranze!)

CINDERELLA:
They're over there, in another room.
They'll be coming soon.
(to herself)
(Farewell to my hopes!)

RAMIRO:
Ma di grazia, voi chi siete?

RAMIRO: *(showing interest in Cinderella)*
But who are you?

CENERENTOLA:
Io chi sono? Eh! Non lo so.

CINDERELLA:
Who am I? I don't know!

RAMIRO:
Nol sapete?

RAMIRO:
You don't know?

CENERENTOLA:
Quasi no. Quel ch'è padre, non è padre.

CINDERELLA:
Well, I sort of know. The man I call father is really my stepfather.

Cinderella becomes befuddled by her explanation and corrects herself.

Onde poi le due sorelle...Era vedova mia madre...Ma fu madre ancor di quelle... Questo padre pien d'orgoglio...

So that my two sisters... My mother was a widow, but she was also the mother of my stepsisters, born of a very proud father.

(Sta'a vedere che m'imbroglio?)
Deh! Scusate, perdonate alla mia semplicità!

(to herself)
(I'm obviously confused.)
Please, excuse me! Forgive my foolishness!

RAMIRO:
(Mi seduce, m'innamora quella sua simplicità.)

RAMIRO:
(Her simplicity seduces and captivates me.)

CLORINDA, TISBE, MAGNIFICO:

Cenerentola...da me!

CLORINDA, TISBE, MAGNIFICO:
(calling from their rooms)
Cinderella, come here!

RAMIRO:
Quante voci! Che cos'è?

RAMIRO:
Whose voices are those?

CENERENTOLA:
A ponente ed a levante. A scirocco e a tramontana. Non ho calma un solo istante, tutto tutto tocca a me.

CINDERELLA:
I'm called from here or there; from near or afar. I never have a moment of peace: I'm expected to do everything for them.

CLORINDA e TISBE:
Cenerentola!

CLORINDA and TISBE:
Cinderella!

CENERENTOLA:
Vengo, vengo! Addio, signore!

CINDERELLA: *(answering her sisters)*
I'm coming! Sir, goodbye!

(Ah ci lascio proprio il core: questo cor più mio non è!)

(to herself, passionately)
(Ah! I'm indeed leaving my heart here: a heart that I can no longer control!)

RAMIRO:
(Quell'accento, quel sembiante è una cosa sovrumana. Io mi perdo in quest'istante già più me non trovo in me.)

RAMIRO:
(How divine her voice is! How beautiful her face! This encounter has made me feel lost; I no longer recognize myself.)

Ramiro becomes rapt in thought as he gazes at Cinderella.

(Che innocenza! Che innocenza! Che candore! Ah! M'invola proprio il core! Questo cor più mio non è.)

(What innocence! What purity! What honesty! She truly has stolen my heart. I no longer control my heart.)

Cinderella exits. Ramiro remains.

RAMIRO:
Non so che dir. Come in sì rozze spoglie. Sì bel volto e gentil!

Ma Don Magnifico non apparisce ancor? Nunziar vorrei del mascherato Principe l'arrivò. Fortunato consiglio! Da semplice scudiero il core dell femmine meglio svelar saprò. Dandini intanto recitando da Principe.

RAMIRO:
I don't know what to say. Her clothing is coarse, but her face is pretty and full of charm.

Why hasn't Don Magnifico arrived yet? Alidoro's advice was excellent: that I disguise myself as a squire, and have my valet Dandini impersonate the prince; in that way, it will be easier to bare these women's hearts.

Don Magnifico enters, dressed in his finest clothes. He approaches Ramiro.

MAGNIFICO:
Domando un milion di perdoni! Dica: e Sua Altezza il Principe?

MAGNIFICO:
A million pardons! Tell me about His Excellency, the Prince?

RAMIRO:
Or ora arriva.

RAMIRO:
He'll be arriving soon.

MAGNIFICO:
E quando?

MAGNIFICO:
When?

RAMIRO:
Tra tre minuti.

RAMIRO:
In about three minutes!

MAGNIFICO:
Tre minuti! Ah figlie!
Sbrigatevi: che serve?
Le vado ad affrettar. Scusi; per queste ragazze benedette. Un secolo è un momento alla toelette.

MAGNIFICO: *(agitated)*
Three minutes! Girls, hurry up!
What's the use? I must go up there to hurry them along. So excuse me; with these damned girls, a moment's primping lasts a century!

Magnifico rushes to his daughter's room.

RAMIRO:
Che buffone!
E Alidoro mio maestro sostien che in queste mura sta la bontà più pura!
Basta, basta, vedrem.
Alle sue figlie convien che m'avvicini.

RAMIRO:
What a buffoon! Nevertheless, my tutor Alidoro maintains that the purest kindness dwells within these walls! Well, we'll find out if that is true. It certainly would behoove me to get to know his daughters better.

Noised are heard outside,

Qual fragor! Non m'inganno.
Ecco Dandini.

What is that noise! If I'm not wrong, it's Dandini.

Courtiers enter, followed by Dandini, disguised as the Prince, then Magnifico, Clorinda, and Tisbe.

CORTIGIANI:
Scegli la sposa, affrettati: s'invola via l'età.
La principesca linea.
Se no s'estinguerà.

COURTIERS: *(addressing Dandini)*
Hurry, choose a bride; time is passing rapidly. If you do not act immediately, the royal lineage will end.

DANDINI:
Come un'ape ne'giorni d'aprile va volando
leggiera e scherzosa; corre al giglio,
poi salta alla rosa, dolce un fiore a cercare per
sé.

DANDINI:
I'm like a bee on a beautiful April day seeking
a sweet flower: flying capriciously and
playfully; darting to the lily, then springing to
the rose.

Fra le belle m'aggiro e rimiro;
ne ho vedute già tante e poi tante ma non trovo
un giudizio, un sembiante, un boccone squisito
per me.

I rove about seeking fair maidens. I have seen
so many, and then some. But I can't seem to
find the combination of brains and beauty that
suits me.

Clorinda and Tisbe appear. Don Magnifico ceremoniiously introduces them to Dandini.

CLORINDA:
Prence!

CLORINDA: *(gushingly)*
Prince!

TISBE:
Sire!

TISBE: *(likewise)*
Sire!

CLORINDA e TISBE:
Ma quanti favori!

CLORINDA and TISBE:
We are so honored that you have considered us!

MAGNIFICO:
Che diluvio! Che abisso di onori!

MAGNIFICO:
It's like a deluge of honors!

DANDINI:
Nulla, nulla; vezzosa; graziosa!

DANDINI: *(to one, and then to the other)*
It's nothing. Such pretty and charming women!

(aside to Ramiro)
(How am I doing?)

(Dico bene? Son tutte papà.)

RAMIRO:
(Bestia! Attento! Ti scosta, va di qua.)

RAMIRO: *(to Dandini)*
(You ass! Be careful! Stay away from me!)

DANDINO:
Per pietà, quelle ciglia abbassate.
Galoppando sen va la ragione, e fra i colpi
d'un doppio cannone spalancato è il mio core
di già.

DANDINI: *(the sisters staring at him longingly)*
For Heaven's sake, lower your eyes! Reason
has abandoned me. You have breached the
fortress of my heart with your eyes, which have
the intensity of a double cannon shot!

(to himself)
(But when our charade is over, tragedy will
reign here!)

(Ma al finir della nostra commedia che
tragedia qui nascer dovrà!)

CLORINDA e TISBE:
(Ei mi guarda. Sospira, delira non v'è dubbio:
è mio schiavo di già.)

CLORINDA and TISBE: *(each to themselves)*
(He's looking at me. He sighs. He is enraptured!
He's already my slave!)

RAMIRO:
(Ah! Perché qui non viene colei, con
quell'aria di grazia e bontà?)

RAMIRO: *(curious if Cinderella is returning)*
(Where is that girl who exuded so much charm
and kindness?)

MAGNIFICO:
(E già cotto, stracotto, spolpato L'Eccellenza si cangia in Maestà.)

MAGNIFICO: *(referring to "Prince" Dandini)*
(He's already smitten, finished. I am now "Your Excellency," soon to become "Your Majesty.")

The Courtiers leave, repeating their advice to Dandini: "Hurry, choose a bride; time is passing by rapidly. If you do not act immediately, the royal lineage will die out."

DANDINI:
Allegrissimamente! Che bel quadri!
Che bocchino che ciglia!
Sieto l'ottava e nona meraviglia.
Già tales patris talem filias.

DANDINI: *(observing Magnifico's daughters)*
Delightful, what lovely images you make! What sweet little mouths, what eyes! You represent the eighth and ninth wonders of the world! Yes, like father, like daughter!

CLORINDA:
Grazie!

CLORINDA: *(bowing)*
Thank you!

MAGNIFICO:
Altezza delle Altezze! Che dice? Mi confonde. Debolezze.

MAGNIFICO: *(also bowing)*
Your Highness of all Highnesses, what are you saying? I'm confused. I feel weak.

DANDINI:
Vere figure etrusche!

DANDINI: *(flatteringly)*
Your daughters are like classic Etruscan figures.

(aside to Ramiro)
(Dico bene?)
(How am I doing?)

RAMIRO:
(Cominci a dirle grosse.)

RAMIRO: *(aside to Dandini)*
(You're beginning to exaggerate.)

DANDINI:
(Io recito da grande, e grande essendo, grande le ho da sparar.)

DANDINI:
(I have to fire off my lines because I'm the main protagonist in an important play.)

MAGNIFICO:
(Bel principotto!
Che non vi fugga: attente.)

MAGNIFICO: *(softly to his daughters)*
(He's a beautiful little prince! Don't let him escape you, so be prudent!)

DANDINI:
Or dunque seguitando quel discorso che non ho cominciato; dai miei lunghi viaggi ritornato e il mio papà trovato, che fra i quondam è capitombolato, e spirando ho ordinato che a vista qual cambiale io sia sposato, o son diseredato.

DANDINI: *(with exaggerated pomposity)*
Now, to continue that speech that I was about to begin. Upon returning from my long travels, I found that my daddy had fallen precipitously into the realm of the late departed, and while he was on his deathbed, he ordered me to get married, or if not, I'd be disinherited.

Fatto ho un invito a tutto il vicinato e trovando un boccone delicato, per me l'ho destinato.

I invited the entire neighborhood to a ball, where I expect to find a delectable young bride.

Ho detto, ho detto, e adesso prendo fiato.

I've said it all, and now I can catch my breath.

MAGNIFICO:
(Che eloquenza norcina!)

MAGNIFICO: *(taken aback, to himself)*
(What erudite, learned eloquence!)

Cinderella enters, dazed by Dandini's elegant attire. Ramiro gazes at her lovingly.

CENERENTOLA:
(Ah! Che bell'abito!)

E quell'altro mi guarda!)

CINDERELLA:
(Oh, what beautiful clothes he wears!
(noticing Ramiro)
And that other man is staring at me!)

RAMIRO:
(Ecco colei! Ma ripalpita il cor.)

RAMIRO:
(There she is! My heart is throbbing again!)

DANDINI:
Belle ragazze. Se vi degnate inciambellare il braccio ai nostri cavalieri, il legno è pronto.

DANDINI: *(to the two sisters)*
Lovely girls, if you deign to do so, allow a cavalier to escort you to the waiting coach.

CLORINDA:
Andiam!

CLORINDA: *(attended by cavaliers)*
Let's go!

TISBE:
Papà, Eccellenza, non tardate a venir!

TISBE:
Daddy, Your Excellency, hurry up! Don't delay!

MAGNIFICO:
Che fai tu qui?
Il cappello e il bastone.

MAGNIFICO: *(irritated by Cinderella's presence)*
What are you doing here?
Bring me my hat and cane!

CENERENTOLA:
Eh, sì Signor!

CINDERELLA:
Yes, sir!

Cinderella hurries to another room)

DANDINI:
Perseguitate presto con i piè baronali i magnifici miei quarti reali?

DANDINI: *(addressing Magnifico)*
Are "Your Baronial feet" ready to follow me to see my magnificent royal quarters?

MAGNIFICO:
Monti in carozza, e vengo.

MAGNIFICO: *(to Dandini)*
Get into your coach and I'll follow right along.

Dandini departs. Magnifico leaves to seek Cinderella.

RAMIRO:
(E pur colei vo' rivider.)

RAMIRO: *(thinking about Cinderella)*
(Yes, I indeed want to see her again!)

MAGNIFICO:
Ma lasciami.

MAGNIFICO: *(from another room,*
Let me alone!

RAMIRO:
(La sgrida?)

RAMIRO:
(He's screaming at her!)

Magnifico re-enters, coat and cane in hand, followed by Cinderella.

CENERENTOLA:
Sentite!

CINDERELLA:
Listen!

MAGNIFICO:
Il tempo vola! Vuoi lasciarmi?

MAGNIFICO:
I'm going to be late! Will you let go of me?

RAMIRO:
(Che vorrà?)

RAMIRO:
(What does she want?)

CENERENTOLA:
Una parola!

CINDERELLA:
Just one word!

(to Magnifico)
Sir, just one word: Take me to the Prince's ball
for just one hour!

Signore, una parola: in casa di quel Principe
un'ora, una'ora sola portatemi a ballar.

MAGNIFICO:
Ha! Ha! Ha!

MAGNIFICO: *(laughing)*
Ha! Ha! Ha!

DANDINI:
(Cos'è? Qui fa la statua?

DANDINI: *(returning, inqluiring of Ramiro)*
(What happened? Why stand there like a statue?)

MAGNIFICO:
La bella Venere! Vezzosa! Pomposetta!
Sguaiata! Covacenere!
Lasciami, deggio andar.

MAGNIFICO: *(derisively, to Cinderella)*
Here's the beautiful Venus! So charming, but
in truth a pompous guttersnipe! Vulgar, lazy
girl! Leave me alone! I must leave!

RAMIRO:
(Silencio ed osserviamo!)

RAMIRO: *(softly to Dandini)*
(Let's be quiet and see what happens!)

DANDINI:
(Ma andiamo o non andiamo?)

DANDINI:
(Are we leaving or not?)

RAMIRO:
(Mi sento lacerar.)

RAMIRO:
(I'm upset by the way he treats her.)

CENERENTOLA:
Ma una mezz'ora, un quarto!

CINDERELLA:
Just for half an hour, a quarter of an hour!

MAGNIFICO:
Ma lasciami o ti stritolo!

MAGNIFICO: *(lifting his cane, threateningly)*
Leave me alone, or I'll beat you to a pulp!

RAMIRO e DANDINI:
Fermate!

RAMIRO and DANDINI: *(restraining Magnifico)*
Stop it!

MAGNIFICO:
Serenissima!

MAGNIFICO: *(bowing to Dandini)*
Most Serene Highness!

Ma vattene!

(turning to Cinderella)
Get lost!

Altezzissima!
Servaccia ignorantissima!

(to Dandini, once again)
Most Exalted Highness!
She's nothing but a lowly, ignorant servant!

RAMIRO e DANDINI:
Serva?

RAMIRO and DANDINI:
A servant?

CENERENTOLA:
Cioè...

CINDERELLA:
That is…

MAGNIFICO:
Vilissima d'un'estrazion bassissima,
vuol far la sufficiente, la cara,
l'avvenente, e non è buona a niente.

Va' in camera, va' in camera la polvere a spazzar.

MAGNIFICO: *(interrupting, covering her lips)*
She's from the lowest background; she wants
to play the darling and beauty, but she's a good
for nothing.
(to Cinderella)
Go into your room and sweep up the dust!

DANDINI:
Ma caro Don Magnifico via, non la
strapazzar.

DANDINI: *(authoritatively)*
My dear Don Magnifico, come now, stop
mistreating her!

RAMIRO:
Or ora la mia collera non posso più frenar.

RAMIRO: *(with repressed scorn)*
I will soon be unable to contain my wrath.

CENERENTOLA:
Ah! Sempre fra la cenera sempre dovrò restar?

Signori, persuadetelo; portatemi a ballar.

CINDERELLA: *(ingenuously)*
Why must I always remain amid the ashes?
(to Ramiro and Dandini)
Gentlemen, persuade him; take me to the ball.

Magnifico breaks free from Cinderella. Alidoro enters, dressed as a beggar, but underneath his disguise he wears a philosopher's garb. He carries a sizable register in his hands.

ALIDORO:
Qui nel mio codice delle zitelle con Don
Magnifico stan tre sorelle.
Or che va il Principe la sposa a scegliere, la
terza figlia io vi domando.

ALIDORO: *(to Magnifico)*
Here is my register of eligible maidens. Don
Magnifico, three sisters live you!
Now that the Prince is about to choose a bride,
I must ask you to let me see your third daughter.

MAGNIFICO:
Che terza figlia mi va figliando?

MAGNIFICO: *(confused)*
A third daughter? Are you trying to make me a
progenitor again?

ALIDORO:
Terza sorella!

ALIDORO:
There's a third sister!

MAGNIFICO:
Ella morì!

MAGNIFICO: *(faking tears)*
She died!

ALIDORO:
Eppur nel codice non v'è così.

ALIDORO:
But my register doesn't indicate that she died.

CENERENTOLA:
(Ah! Di me parlano.)

No, non morì!

CINDERELLA: *(to herself)*
(They're talking about me.)
(Cinderella advances naively.)
No, she didn't die!

MAGNIFICO:
Sta' zitta lì!

MAGNIFICO: *(to Cinderella)*
Be quiet!

ALIDORO:
Guardate qui!

ALIDORO:
Now look here!

MAGNIFICO:
Se tu respiri, ti scanno qui.

MAGNIFICO: *(pushing Cinderella away)*
If you as much as breathe, I'll slash your throat!

RAMIRO, DANDINI, ALIDORO:
Dunque morì?

RAMIRO, DANDINI, ALIDORO:
She died?

MAGNIFICO:
Altezza sì!

MAGNIFICO: *(to Dandini)*
Your Highness, she died!

There is a prolonged silence.

TUTTI:
Nel volto estatico di questo e quello si legge il vortice del lor cervello, che ondeggia e dubita e incerto sta.

ALL:
The faces of this one and that one are ecstatic, but one can read that their minds are confused; they waver because of doubt and uncertainty.

MAGNIFICO:
Se tu più mormori solo una sillaba un cimiterio que si farà.

MAGNIFICO: *(menacingly to Cinderella)*
One more word out of you and this house will be your cemetery!

CENERENTOLA:
Deh soccorretemi, deh non lasciatemi. Ah! Di me misera che mai sarà?

CINDERELLA: *(passionately)*
Help me, please don't leave me! What will become of my wretched soul?

RAMIRO:
Via consolatevi!

RAMIRO: *(to Cinderella)*
Come, cheer up!

Signor lasciatela!

(to Magnifico)
Sir, leave her alone!

(Già la mia furia crescendo va.)

(to himself)
(I'm becoming more and more enraged.)

ALIDORO:
Via meno strepito: fate silenzio, o qualche scandolo qui nascerà.

ALIDORO: *(moving between them)*
Come, be quiet and less noise, or you will cause a scandal to erupt.

DANDINI:
Io sono un Principe, o sono un cavolo? Vi mando al diavolo!

DANDINI: *(to Magnifico)*
Am I a prince, or am I some cabbage? I'm sending you to the devil!

Venite qua!

(to Cinderella)
Come here!

Dandini pulls Magnifico away from Cinderella. Cinderella runs to her room and shuts the door. A moment later Alidoro enters, disguised as a beggar.

ALIDORO:
Sì, tutto cangerà. Quel folle orgoglio poca polve sarà, gioco del vento; e al tenero lamento succederà il sorriso. Figlia, figlia...

ALIDORO: *(to Cinderella)*
Yes, everything will change. Your stepsister's mad pride, will turn to dust. And after all of your suffering, you will indeed smile once again. My daughter...

CENERENTOLA:
Figlia voi mi chiamate? O questa è bella! Il padrigno Barone non vuole essermi padre; e voi, peraltro, guardando i stracci vostri e i stracci miei, degna d'un padre tal figlia sarei.

CINDERELLA: *(expressing surprise)*
Did you call me daughter? Now that's a good one! The Baron, my stepfather, doesn't want to be called father. And looking at the two of us in rags, I would be a worthy daughter to you.

ALIDORO:
Taci, figlia, e vieni meco!

ALIDORO:
Be quiet, my daughter, and come with me!

CENERENTOLA:
Teco, e dove?

CINDERELLA:
Go with you? Where?

ALIDORO:
Del Principe al festino!

ALIDORO:
To the Prince's ball!

CENERENTOLA:
Tu mi vieni a burlar?
Con questi stracci? Come Paris e Vienna?
Oh che bell'ambo.

CINDERELLA:
Are you making fun of me?
In these rags? We don't quite have the elegance of a Paris or Vienna.

ALIDORO:
No! Sublima il pensiero!
Abiti, gioie, tutto avrete da me.
Fasto, richezza non v'abbaglino il cor.
Dama sarete; scoprirvi non dovrete.
Amor soltanto tutto v'insegnerà.
E se dubit ancor, mira chi sono!

ALIDORO:
No! Let your thoughts vanish!
Everything has changed for you! Instead of mud, your feet will stand on treasures!
You will be a lady. Come with me and don't be afraid! I will teach you all about love.
And if you still have doubt, behold who I am!

Alidoro sheds his beggar's clothes and reveals himself:
a handsome, well-dressed Philosopher.

Là del ciel nell'arcano profundo, del poter sull'altissimo Trono veglia un Nume, signor del mondo, al cui piè basso mormora il tuono.

There, in Heaven's mysterious depths, an omnipotent God sits on His high throne, Lord of the world; at His feet even thunder rumbles feebly.

Tutto sa, tutto vede, e non lascia nell'ambascia perir la bontà.
Fra la cenere, il pianto, l'affano, ei ti vede, o fanciulla innocente. Non temer, si è cambiata la scena: la tua pena cangiando già va.

He knows everything. He sees everything, and He will not permit goodness to die in sorrow.
Innocent young girl, He sees you among the cinders, and He sees your tears. Don't be afraid; your pain has transformed into happiness.

S'ode avvicinarsi una carozza. Un crescente mormorio non ti sembra d'ascoltar? Ah sta' lieta: è il cocchio mio su cui voli a trionfar.

Listen for my coach. Do you hear its sounds approaching? Be joyous: it shall hasten you to triumph!

Tu mi guardi, ti confondi.
Ehi ragazza, non rispondi?
sconcertata è la tua testa e rimbalza qua e là, come nave in gran tempesta che di sotto in su sen va.

Why do you look at me in bewilderment?
Young lady, aren't you going to answer me?
I realize that your mind is confounded, swinging back and forth, like a storm-tossed ship plunging in and out of the waves.

Ma già il nembo è terminato, scintillò serenità.
Il destino s'è cangiato, l'innocenza brillerà!

But now the storm is over, and a scintillating serenity will be your fate. Innocence shall triumph!

Alidoro leads Cinderella to his waiting coach.

*The study of Ramiro's palace, Dandini enters with Clorinda and Tisbe on either arm,
followed by Magnifico, Ramiro and Courtiers.)*

DANDINI:
Ma bravo, bravo, bravo! Caro il mio Don
Magnifico! Di vigne, di vendemmie e di vino
m'avete fatto una disertazione, lodo il vostro talento.

Si vede che ha studiato.

Si porti sui momento dove sta il nostro vino
conservato e se sta saldo e intrepido al
trigesimo assaggio lo promovo all'onor di
cantiniero io distinguo i talenti e premio il
saggio.

MAGNIFICO:
Prence! L'Altezza Vostra è un pozzo di bontà.
Più se ne resta a cavar!

(Figlie! Vedete? Non regge al vostro merto;
n'è la mia promozion indizio certo.)

Clorinduccia! Tisbina! Tenete allegro il Re.
Vado in cantina.

DANDINI:
Well done, my dear Don Magnifico.
You've given me a dissertation about vineyards,
harvests and wines. I salute your talent!

(to Ramiro)
One can see that he has done his homework.

(to Magnifico and the Courtiers)
Take him immediately to our wine cellars! If
he remains steady and erect after the thirteenth
tasting, I will promote him to the honorable post
of vintner. I have an eye for talent and I reward
wisdom.

MAGNIFICO:
Prince! Your Highness is a wellspring of
kindness: your graciousness never ceases!

(softly, to his daughters)
(Girls, did you see that? He can't resist you, so
he has appointed me his vintner.)

(aloud, with exaggerated unctuousness)
Little Clorinda! Sweet Tisbe! Keep the king
happy! I am off to the wine cellar!

Don Magnifico exits, en route to the wine cellars.

RAMIRO:
(Esamina, disvela, e fedelmente tutto mi
narrerai.)

(Anch'io fra poco il cor ne tenterò; del volto i
vezzi svaniscon con l'età, ma il core...)

DANDINI:
(Il core credo che sia un melon tagliato a fette;
un timballo l'ingegno, e il cervello una casa
spigionata.)
Il mio volere ha forza d'un editto.
Eseguite trottanto il cenno mio.
Udiste?

RAMIRO:
Udii!

DANDINI:
Fido vassallo, addio!

RAMIRO: *(whispering to Dandini)*
(Keep an eye on him and faithfully report
everything to me.)

(referring to Clorinda)
(Also, I intend to test her heart very shortly;
beauty fades with age, but the heart...)

DANDINI: *(referring to Magnifico)*
(I believe his heart is a sliced melon; the brain
of a kettle-drum, and as empty as a vacant
house.)
My will has the strength of an edict.
Carry out my orders expeditiously!
Did you hear me?

RAMIRO:
I heard you!

DANDINI: *(dismissing Ramiro)*
Farewell, faithful vassal!

After Ramiro departs, Dandini turns his attention to Clorinda and Tisbe.

Ora sono da voi. Scommetterei che siete fatte al torno e che il guercetto amore è stato il tornitore.

Now back to you two. I'll bet that you were fashioned at a celestial lathe; and Cupid himself was doing the turning.

CLORINDA:
Con permesso! (La maggiore son io, onde la prego darmi la preferenza.)

CLORINDA: *(grabbing Dandini's arm)*
Pardon me! (I am the older of the two, and I think I deserve preference.)

TISBE:
Con sua buona licenza!(La minore son io. M'invecchierò più tardi.)

TISBE: *(also grabbing Dandini's arm)*
With your permission!(I am the younger one. It will be a long time before begin to age.)

CLORINDA:
Scusi! (Quella è fanciulla. Proprio non sa di nulla.)

CLORINDA: *(interrupting)*
Pardon me! (She is a mere child, who really knows nothing.)

TISBE:
Permetta! (Quella è un'acqua sensa sale, non fa né ben né male.)

TISBE:
Permit me! (My sister is the very quintessence of tastelessness: a good for nothing.)

CLORINDA:
Di grazia! (I dritti miei la prego bilanciar.)

CLORINDA:
Pardon me! (I implore you to heed my rights.)

TISBE:
Perdoni! (Veda, io non tengo rosetto.)

TISBE:
Pardon me! (I don't have to wear rouge.)

CLORINDA:
Ascolti! (Quel suo bianco è di bianchetto.)

CLORINDA:
Listen! (That pallor of hers is pure white gloss.)

TISBE:
Senta!

TISBE:
Listen!

CLORINDA:
Mi favorisca!

CLORINDA:
Take me!

DANDINI:
Anime belle! Mi volete spaccar? Non dubitate. Ho due occhi reali e non adopro occhiali.

DANDINI: *(breaking away from them)*
My dears, are you trying to tear me apart? Don't forget, that I have perfect eyesight, and I do not have to wear eyeglasses.

(Fidati pur di me, mio caro ogetto!)

(to Clorinda)
(Trust me!)

(Per te sola mi batte il core in petto.)

(to Tisbe)
(My heart beats for you alone.)

TISBE:
M'inchino a Vostr' Altezza.

TISBE: *(ironically bowing to her sister)*
I bow to Your Highness.

CLORINDA:
Anzi all'Altezza Vostra!

CLORINDA: *(likewise bowing)*
To Your Supreme Highness!

TISBE:
Verrò a portarle qualche memoriale!

TISBE: *(sarcastically)*
I'll be sure to answer your prayers!

CLORINDA:
Lectum!

CLORINDA:
Ditto!

TISBE:
Ce la vedremo!

TISBE:
We'll see!

CLORINDA:
Forse sì, forse no!

CLORINDA:
Maybe yes, maybe no!

TISBE:
Poter del mondo!

TISBE:
By Jove!

CLORINDA:
Le faccio riverenza!

CLORINDA: *(bowing very low)*
I'll revere you!

TISBE:
Oh! Mi sprofondo!

TISBE:
I bow with the most profound respect!

*A drawing room in Prince Ramiro's palace. There is a table with writing materials.
Don Magnifico, the Prince's new vintner, wears a coat embroidered with grapes.
He is surrounded by Courtiers.*

CORTIGIANI:
Trenta botti già gusto! E bevuto ha già per tre
e finor non barcollò!
È piaciuto a Sua Maestà nominarlo cantinier.
Intendente dei bicchier con estesa autorità.
Presidente al vendemmiar.
Direttor dell'evoè;
onde tutti intorno a te s'affolliamo qui a saltar.

COURTIERS:
He has tasted thirty barrels of wine. drunk
enough for three, and hasn't begun to stagger!
His majesty was delighted to name him vintner:
Superintendent of Wine Glasses, with extended
authority as President of the Grape Harvest, and
also Director of Bacchic Festivities.
We are all thrilled by your appointment!

MAGNIFICO:
Intendente! Direttor! Presidente! Cantinier!
Grazie, grazie, che piacer!
Che girandola ho nel cor.
Si venga a scrivere quel che dettiamo.
Sei mila copie poi ne vogliamo.

MAGNIFICO:
Superintendent! Director! President! Vintner!
Thank you. What pleasure!
I feel my heart pounding rapidly!
Write down what I am about to dictate;
I will want six thousand copies of it distributed!

The Courtiers seat themselves around the table, poised to beging writing.

CORTIGIANI:
Già pronti a scrivere tutti siam qui.

COURTIERS:
We are ready to write down everything you say.

MAGNIFICO:
"Noi Don Magnifico..."
Questo in maiuscole.

MAGNIFICO:
"We...Don Magnifico..."
Put that in capital letters!

Bravi! Così!

(The men re-write and use capital letters.)
Bravo! That's it!

"Noi, Don Magnifico, Duca e Barone dell'antichissimo Montefiascone; Grand'intendente; Gran presidente, con gli altri titoli..." con venti etcetera,
"di nostra propria autorità, riceva l'ordine chi leggerà, di più non mescere per anni quindici nel vino amabile d'acqua una gocciola. Alias capietur et stranguletur perché ita..."etcetera, "laonde..." etcetera.

"We...Don Magnifico, Duke and Baron of the ancient town of Montefiascone; great superintendent, great president..." with twenty etceteras,
"and exercising absolute authority, receives this decree, which will read as follows: For the next fifteen years, let no one dare mix a single drop of water into a bottle of good wine, lest he be caught and strangled. ..." etcetera.

CORTIGIANI:
Barone, etcetera; è fatto già!

(COURTIERS:
Baron, etcetera, and it is done!

Magnifico signs the decree.

MAGNIFICO:
Ora affiggetelo per la città!

MAGNIFICO:
Now post it all over town!

CORTIGIANI:
Il pranzo in ordine. Andiamo a mettere vino a diluvio si beverà.

COURTIERS:
We'll check to see that dinner is being prepared; at dinner, we'll drink wine as if it were water.

MAGNIFICO:
Premio bellissimo di piastre sedici a chi più Malaga si succhierà.

MAGNIFICO:
And a most handsome prize of sixteen *piastres* to the one who drinks the most Malaga wine.

The Courtiers and Don Magnifico exit. Dandini and Ramiro appear, looking about cautiously.

RAMIRO:
Zitto, zitto, piano, piano; senza strepito e rumore; delle due qual è l'umore?
Esattezza e verità!

RAMIRO: *(softly)*
Quietly! Don't make any noise! Describe the character of those two sisters?
Be detailed and truthful!

DANDINI:
Sotto voce a mezzo tuono; in estrema confidenza: sono un misto d'insolenza, di capriccio e vanità

DANDINI:
IN half voice, and in extreme confidence, they are a combination of insolence, conceit and vanity.

RAMIRO:
E Alidoro mi dicea che una figlia del Barone...

RAMIRO:
Alidoro told me that one of the Baron's daughters...

DANDINI:
Eh! Il maestro ha un gran testone. Oca eguale non si dà.
(Son due vere banderuole...mi conviene dissimular.)

DANDINI:
Your tutor is hardheaded: a simpleton without equal.
(Both of them are fickle and inconstant. Nevertheless, we must continue our charade.)

RAMIRO:
(Se le sposi pur chi vuole...seguitiamo a recitar.)

RAMIRO:
Anyone who wants to marry them can have them! Let's continue playing our roles.)

Clorinda and Tisbe enter the room, each from different doors.

CLORINDA:
Principino dove siete?

CLORINDA:
Little Prince, where are you?

TISBE:
Principino dove state?

TISBE:
Little Prince, where can you be?

CLORINDA e TISBE:
Ah! Perché mi abbandonate? Mi farete
disperare.

CLORINDA and TISBE:
Why have you abandoned me? You'll make me
surrender to despair.

CLORINDA:
Io vi voglio...

CLORINDA:
I want you...

TISBE:
Vi vogl'io...

TISBE:
I want you...

DANDINI:
Ma non diamo in bagattelle. Maritarsi a due
sorelle tutte insieme non si può! Una sposo.

DANDINI: *(addressing both sisters)*
Let's not concern ourselves with trifles: I can't
marry both of you, but I can marry one of you.

CLORINDA, TISBE:
E l'altra?

CLORINDA, then TISBE: *(eagerly)*
And the other one?

DANDINI:
All'amico la darò.

DANDINI: *(indicating Ramiro)*
I'll give the other one to my friend over here.

CLORINDA e TISBE:
No no no no no, un scudiero! Questo no!

CLORINDA and TISBE:
Good Heavens! Not to a squire!

RAMIRO:
Sarò docile, amoroso, tenerissimo di cuore!

RAMIRO: *(between them, with sweetness)*
I will be obedient, loving and tender!

CLORINDA e TISBE:
Un scudiero! No signore. Un scudiero! Questo no!

CLORINDA and TISBE: *(disdainfully)*
A squire! No! A squire! Not that!

CLORINDA:
Con un'anima plebèa!

CLORINDA:
With a plebeian soul!

TISBE:
Con un'aria dozzinale!

TISBE:
With the manners of a commoner!

CLORINDA e TISBE:
Mi fa male, mi fa male solamente a immaginar.

CLORINDA and TISBE: *(pretentiously)*
It makes me sick just imagining such a union.

DANDINI, RAMIRO:
(La scenetta è originale veramente da contar.)

DANDINI, RAMIRO: *(to themselves)*
(This is a comedy worthy of retelling.)

Cavaliers and Alidoro enter.

CAVALIERI:
Venga, inoltri, avanzi il piè.
Anticamera non v'è.

CAVALIERS: *(referring to a veiled woman)*
Let her come inside. There's no need for her to
wait in the anteroom.

RAMIRO e DANDINI:
Sapientissimo Alidoro, questo strepito cos'è?

RAMIRO and DANDINI: *(to Alidoro)*
Most wise Alidoro, what is all that noise about?

ALIDORO:
Dama incognita qua vien. Sopra il volta un velo tien.

ALIDORO:
An unknown lady has come here; her face is covered by a veil.

CLORINDA e TISBE:
Una dama!

CLORINDA and TISBE:
A lady!

ALIDORO:
· Signor sì!

ALIDORO:
Yes sir!

CLORINDA e TISBE:
Ma chi è?

CLORINDA and TISBE:
Who can she be?

ALIDORO:
Nol palesò.

ALIDORO:
She didn't reveal her name.

CLORINDA e TISBE:
Sarà bella?

CLORINDA and TISBE:
Is she beautiful?

DANDINI e RAMIRO:
Chi sarà?

DANDINI and RAMIRO:
Who can she be?

ALIDORO:
Sì e no.

ALIDORO:
No one knows.

CLORINDA:
Non parlò?

CLORINDA:
Did she say anything?

ALIDORO:
Signora no.

ALIDORO:
No, Madam.

TISBE:
E qui vien?

TISBE:
Why has she come here?

ALIDORO:
Chi sa perché?

ALIDORO:
No one knows why.

TUTTI:
Chi sarà? Chi è? Perché?
Non si sa. Si vedrà.

ALL:
Who might she be? Who is it? Why? We don't know, but soon we'll find out.

There is a long moment of silent introspection.

CLORINDA e TISBE:
(Gelosia già già mi lacera, già il cervel più in me non è.)

CLORINDA and TISBE: *(softly)*
(Jealousy now tears me apart! I am going out of my mind!)

ALIDORO:
(Gelosia già già le rosica, più il cervello in lor non è.)

ALIDORO: *(thinking about the two sisters)*
(Jealousy is already gnawing at them. They're going out of their minds.)

RAMIRO:
Un ignoto arcano palpito ora m'agita, perché?

RAMIRO: *(thinking about the woman)*
(A strange, mysterious passion stirs inside. Why?)

DANDINI:
(Diventato son di zucchero: quante mosche intorno a me.)

DANDINI: *(commenting about the others)*
(I must have turned into sugar! Look at how many flies are buzzing around me!)

At a signal from Dandini, Alidoro, Courtiers and ladies-in-waiting escort the unknown woman into the room. The unknown woman is Cinderella, elegantly attired, with her face covered by a veil.

CORO:
Ah! Se velata ancor, dal seno il cor ci ha tolto, se svelerai quel volto che sarà?

CHORUS:
You are veiled, but you have stolen our hearts. What would happen if you reveal your face?

CENERENTOLA:
Sprezzo quei don che versa fortuna capricciosa. M'offra chi mi vuol sposa, rispetto, amor, bontà.

CINDERELLA:
I despise capriciousness and insincerity; the man who wants me for a bride only needs to offer me respect, love and kindness.

RAMIRO:
(Di quella voce il suono ignoto al cor non scende; perché la speme accende? Di me maggior mi fa.)

RAMIRO: *(to himself)*
(I recognize that voice; it reaches into my heart; it kindles hope; it transforms me into a more noble man.)

DANDINI:
Begli occhi che dal velo vibrate un raggio acuto, svelatevi un minuto almen per civiltà!

DANDINI:
The lovely eyes behind that veil radiate. As a courtesy, reveal yourself for but one minute!

CLORINDA e TISBE:
(Vedremo il gran miracolo di questa rarità!)

CLORINDA and TISBE: *(to themselves)*
(Let's see the miracle of this rare beauty!)

Cinderella removes her veil. Everyone recognizes her; they are all surprised and stunned. As they stare at Cinderella, each comments his astonishment to himself; Cinderella gazes fixedly at Ramiro.

TUTTI:
(Ah! Parlar - pensar - vorrei. Parlar - pensar - non so. Questo è un inganno/è un incanto, o dei! Quel volto mi atterrò.)

ALL:
(Ah! I can neither speak nor think. This must be some kind of chicanery and deceit. God, that face has smitten me!)

ALIDORO:
(Parlar - pensar - vorrebbe. Parlar - pensar - non può. Amar già la dovrebbe, il colpo no non sbagliò.)

ALIDORO: *(to himself, about Prince Ramiro)*
(I can neither speak nor think.
My ruse did not fail: he must already be in love with her.)

MAGNIFICO:
Signor Altezza, è in tavola!

MAGNIFICO: *(to Dandini)*
My Lord, Your Highness, dinner is served!

(Catching sight of Cinderella)

Che...co...chi...sì...che bestia! Quando si dice i simili! Non sembra Cenerentola?

What...how...who...yes...what! Speaking of resemblances, doesn't she look like Cinderella?

CLORINDA e TISBE:
Pareva ancora a noi, ma a riguardarla poi,
la nostra è goffa e attratta.
Questa è un po' più ben fatta;
ma poi non è una Venere
da farci spaventar.

CLORINDA and TISBE:
She seemed so to us, but after a second look,
we concluded that our Cinderella is clumsier
and more awkward. This girl is a bit more
attractive; nevertheless, she's not some Venus
that would jeopardize our chances.

MAGNIFICO:
Quella sta nella cenera;
ha stracci sol per abiti.

MAGNIFICO:
Cinderella is at home among the ashes,
and besides, she only has rags to wear.

CENERENTOLA:
(Il vecchio guarda e dubita.)

CINDERELLA: *(thinking about Magnifico)*
(The old man is staring at me skeptically.)

RAMIRO:
(Mi guarda, e par che palpiti.)

RAMIRO:
(She looks at me; it seems her heart beats faster.)

DANDINI:
Ma non facciam le statue.
Patisce l'individuo: andiamo presto in tavola.
Poi balleremo il Taice,
e quindi la bellissima,
con me s'ha da sposar!

DANDINI:
Let's not stand about like statues, or we'll
develop hunger pangs. Let's go to the dinner
table, and afterwards, we'll dance the *Taice*
(country dance)! And then I'll pick the fairest
as my bride!

TUTTI (meno Dandini)
Andiamo, andiamo a tavola. Si voli a giubilar.

ALL (Except Dandini):
Let's go quickly to dine and indulge ourselves!

DANDINI:
(Oggi che fo da Principe per quattro io
vuo'mangiar!)

DANDINI: *(to himself)*
(Today, since I'm acting the role of Prince, I
want to eat enough for four people!)

TUTTI:
Mi par d'essere sognando fra giardini e fra
boschetti; i ruscelli sussurrando, gorgheggiando
gli augelletti, in un mare di delizie fanno
l'anima nuotar.

ALL:
I seem to be dreaming that I'm standing in
gardens and groves: the babbling brooks and
chirping of little birds make my spirit seem to
swim in a sea of happiness and pleasure.

Ma ho timor che sotto terra piano piano a poco a
poco si sviluppi un certo foco. E improvviso a
tutti ignoto balzi fuori un terremoto, che crollando,
strepitando fracassando, sconquassando.
Poi mi venga a risvegliar. E ho paura che il mio
sogno vada in fumo a dileguar.

But I fear that beneath me a fire is starting to
smolder. And suddenly, without realizing it, an
earthquake erupts. Its smashing, roaring,
shaking and crashing has awakened me,
arousing my fear that my dream will end up in
smoke and vanish.

END of ACT I

ACT II

A room in Prince Ramiro's palace. Cinderella appears, followed by Magnifico,
with Clorinda and Tisbe on his arms.

CORO:
Ah! Della bella incognita; l'arrivo inaspettato
peggior assai del fulmine per certe ninfe è
stato.

CORO:
For those two beauties, Clorinda and Tisbe, the
sudden arrival of the mysterious, unknown lady
was worse than a striking lightning bolt.

MAGNIFICO:
Mi par che quei birbanti ridessero di noi
sottocappotto. Corpo del mosto cotto, fo un
cavaliericidio.

MAGNIFICO:
They look at her and grumble. They smile at
her, but they shudder within. There is a grating
in their hearts that is consuming them alive.

TISBE:
Papà, non v'inquietate!

TISBE:
Papa, don't fret!

MAGNIFICO:
Ho nella testa quattro mila pensieri. Ci
mancava quella madama anonima.

MAGNIFICO:
I have four numerous thoughts running through
my head. We'd be better off without the
appearance of that unknown woman.

CLORINDA:
E credete che del Principe il core ci contrasti?
Somiglia Cenerentola e vi basta.

CLORINDA:
Do you think she's our rival for the Prince's
heart? She resembles Cinderella, but that's the
extent of it.

MAGNIFICO:
Somiglia tanto e tanto che son due gocce
d'acqua.

MAGNIFICO: *(promenading back and forth)*
She resembles her to the extent that they're as
identical as two drops of water.

E quando a pranzo faceva un certo verso è lei,
con la bocca, brontolavo fra me: per Bacco,
ma come dagli Ebrei,

At the dinner table, when she made a certain
movement with her mouth, I grumbled to
myself, "by Jove it's her!"

prender l'abito a nolo!
Aver coraggio di venire fra noi e poi parlar
coi linci a squinci? E poi starsene con sì gran
disinvoltura e non temere una schiaffeggiatura?

Imagine, she rented those clothes and then had
the gall to come here and speak in that high
falutin language? And, she haughtily paraded
about, unafraid that I might slap her in the face.

TISBE:
Già, già questa figliastra fino in chi la
somiglia è a noi funesta!

TISBE:
Her resemblance to Cinderella could be disaster
for us!

MAGNIFICO:
Ma tu sai che tempesta mi piomberebbe
addosso, se scuopre alcun come ho dilapidato
il patrimonio suo!

MAGNIFICO:
More importantly, you do know what a scandal
there would be if someone found out that I
have squandered her inheritance!

Per abbigliarvi, al verde l'ho ridotto.
È diventato un vero sacco d'ossa. Ah se si
scopre, avrei trovato il resto del carlino.

CLORINDA:
E paventar potete a noi vicino?

MAGNIFICO:
Vi son buone speranze?

CLORINDA:
Eh! Niente, niente!

TISBE:
Posso dir ch'è certezza.

CLORINDA:
Io quasi quasi potrei dar delle cariche!

TISBE:
In segreto mi ha detto: anima mia, ha fatto un
gran sospiro, è andato via.

CLORINDA:
Un sospiro cos'è?
Quando mi vede subito ride.

MAGNIFICO:
Ah! Dunque qui sospira, e qui ride.

CLORINDA:
Dite, papà Barone, voi che avete un testone.
Qual è il vostro pensier? Ditelo schietto.

MAGNIFICO:
Giocato ho un ambo e vincerò l'eletto. Da voi
due non si scappa; c'intenderem fra noi;
viscere mie, mi raccomando a voi.

Quest'è il tempo opportuno per rimettermi in
piedi. Lo sapete io sono indebitato. Fino i
stivali a tromba ho ipotecato.

Ma che flusso e riflusso avrò di memoriali!
Ah, questo solo è il paterno desio, che facciate
il rescritto a modo mio. C'intenderem fra noi.
Viscere mie, mi raccomando a voi.

Sia qualunque delle figlie che fra poco andrà
sul trono. Ah! Non lasci in abbandono un
magnifico papà.

I spent all of her inheritance to keep you girls
in fine clothes, and in the process, she became
a real bag of bones.

CLORINDA: *(with a mysterious look)*
How can you be so afraid when we are here,
close to you?

MAGNIFICO:
Is there any hope?

CLORINDA:
I don't think so!

TISBE:
It seems a certainty to me!

CLORINDA:
I could almost give it another try!

TISBE:
In secret, he said to me: "My beloved," but then
he made a big sigh and left.

CLORINDA:
A sigh! What is that?
When he sees me, he smiles right away.

MAGNIFICO: *(looking at one, then the other)*
Then for you he sighs, and for you he smiles.

CLORINDA:
Tell me, daddy Baron, who possesses such a
big brain. What do you think? Tell me bluntly!

MAGNIFICO:
If I bet on my two daughters, I'll emerge a
winner. He can't escape from both of you. Your
blessed fate will be grist for the gossip papers!

This may be a perfect opportunity for me to
get back up on my feet. You know that I'm
heavily in debt; I've even pawned my boots.

I'll have quite a rush of marriage proposals!
My one wish is that one of you will marry the
Prince, which will save me. You, my daughters,
the fruits of my loins, I place my trust in you!

But whichever one of you girls ascends the
throne; do not abandon such a wonderful father
as me!

Già mi par che questo e quello, conficcandomi
a un cantone e cavandosi il cappello,
incominci: sor Barone; alla figlia sua reale
porterebbe un memoriale?
Prende poi la cioccolata, e una doppia ben
coniata faccia intanto scivolar.

I already see this person or that person pushing
me into a corner, doffing his hat and saying:
"My lord Baron, would you kindly take this
marriage petition to your royal daughter?
In appreciation, please accept this well minted
doubloon!"

Io rispondo: eh sì, vedremo. Già è di peso?
Parleremo, da palazzo può passar.
Mi rivolto: e vezzosetta, tutta odori e tutta
unguenti, mi s'inchina una scuffietta fra
sospiri e complimenti: Baroncino! Si ricordi
quell'affare.

Daughters! Understand me: without money you
are speaking to the deaf! I will be surrounded
by the aromas of pomades of charming women,
who wear little bonnets. They will sigh,
compliment me and bow respectfully: "Little
Baron! Remember that matter."

E già m'intende; sensa argento parla ai sordi.
La manina alquanto stende, fa una piastra
sdrucciolar. Io galante: occhietti bei! Ah! Per
voi che non farei io vi voglio contentar!

A woman will hold out her frail hand, causing
a piaster to drop. I, the gallant, say: "Lovely
eyes! Ah! For you there is nothing I wouldn't
do! I want to help you!"

Mi risveglio a mezzi giorno: suono appena il
campanello, che mi vedo al letto intorno
supplichevole drappello.

I will sleep every day until noon, and never have
to ring the bell for my breakfast, or call my
valet to bring me my clothes.

Questo cerca protezione; quello ha torto e
vuol ragione; chi vorrebbe un impieguccio;
chi una cattedra ed è un ciuccio;
chi l'appalto delle spille, chi la pesca
dell'anguille.

Petitioners will gather: this one seeks
protection; that one has been wronged and
wishes redress; another seeks a nice job; an
idiot a professorship; another a monopoly for
brooches, and another of eels.

Ed intanto in ogni lato sarà zeppo e contornato
di memorie e petizioni, di galline, di sturioni,
di bottiglie, di broccati, di candele e marinati,
di ciambelle e pasticcetti, di canditi e di
confetti, di piastroni, di dobloni, di vaniglia e
di caffè.

Meanwhile from all sides there are petitions,
for chickens and sturgeons, for bottles, for
brocades, for candles and marinated pickles,
for doughnuts and pies, for candied fruit and
sugared almonds, for heavy pastries and
doubloons, for vanilla and for coffee.

Basta, basta non portate!
Terminate, ve n'andate? Serro l'uscio a
catenaccio. Importuni, seccatori, fuori fuori,
via da me!

Enough, enough! Don't bring me anything else!
Stop already! Go away! I shall lock the door
with a heavy chain. Annoying people, pests, out,
away from me. Quickly, out of here!

Magnifico leaves, followed by Clorinda and Tisbe.
Soon after, Ramiro enters, followed by Cinderella, who is fleeing from Dandini.
Then Alidoro appears.

RAMIRO:

Ah! Questa bella incognita con quella
somiglianza all'infelice, che mi colpi stamane
mi va destando in petto certa ignota permura.
Anche Dandini mi sembra innamorato.

RAMIRO:

This lovely, unknown woman, who resembles
that wretched one, struck me this morning; she
has awakened a mysterious yearning in my heart.
Even Dandini seems to be in love with her.

Eccoli: udirli or qui potrò celato.

They're coming! I'll hide there, where I can
overhear their conversation.

Ramiro hides. He observes Cinderella fleeing from Dandini.
Alidoro also remains aside, observing them.

DANDINI:
Ma non fuggir, per Bacco! Quattro volte mi
hai fatto misurar la galleria.

DANDINI: *(trying to catch up with Cinderella)*
By Jove, don't dash off like that! You've made
me trek back and forth in the gallery four times.

CENERENTOLA:
O mutate linguaggio, o vado via.

CINDERELLA:
Either you change the subject or I'll go away.

DANDINI:
Ma che? Il parlar d'amore è forse una
stoccata!

DANDINI:
Why? Is telling you that I love you such a bad
thing?

CENERENTOLA:
Ma io d'un altro sono innamorata!

CINDERELLA:
I am in love with another man!

DANDINI:
E mi lo dice in faccia?

DANDINI:
You dare say that to my face?

CENERENTOLA:
Ah! Mio signore. Deh! Non andate in collera
col mio labbro sincero.

CINDERELLA:
My lord, please don't get angry. I speak to you
with sincerity.

DANDINI:
Ed ami?

DANDINI:
Who are you in love with?

CINDERELLA:
Scusi!

CINDERELLA:
Forgive me!

DANDINI:
Ed ami?

DANDINI:
Who are you in love with?

CENERENTOLA:
Il suo scudiero!

CINDERELLA:
Your squire!

RAMIRO:
Oh gioia! Anima mia!

RAMIRO: *(revealing himself)*
What joy! My beloved!

ALIDORO:
(Va a meraviglia!)

ALIDORO: *(showing his approval)*
(It's going marvelously well!)

RAMIRO:
Ma il grado e la ricchezza non seduce il tuo core!

RAMIRO:
Rank and riches do not seduce your heart?

CENERENTOLA:
Mio fasto è la virtù, ricchezza è amore!

CINDERELLA:
My wealth is my virtue: that wealth is love!

RAMIRO:
Dunque saresti mia?

RAMIRO:
Then you would be mine?

CENERENTOLA:
Piano, tu devi pria ricercarmi, conoscermi,
vedermi, esaminar la mia fortuna!

CINDERELLA:
Take it easy! First learn about me and get to
know me: get to know my qualities!

RAMIRO:
Io teco, cara, verrò volando.

RAMIRO:
I shall hasten to you, my dearest.

CENERENTOLA:
Fermati: non seguirmi. Il te'l comando!

CINDERELLA:
But don't follow me!

RAMIRO:
E come dunque?

RAMIRO:
Why not?

CENERENTOLA:
Tieni. Cercami; e alla mia destra il compagno
vedrai.
E allor, se non ti spaccio, allor m'avrai.

CINDERELLA: *(giving him a bracelet)*
Here, the bracelet's companion will be on my
right hand.
When you find me, if I still please you, then I
will be yours.

Cinderella leaves.

RAMIRO:
Dandini, che ne dici?

RAMIRO:
Dandini, what do you say to that?

DANDINI:
Eh! Dico che da Principe sono passato a far da
testimonio.

DANDINI:
I'd say that after having been a prince, I've
become a witness.

RAMIRO:
E allor, "se non ti spaccio, allor m'avrai."
Quali enigmi son questi?

RAMIRO:
And then, "if I still please you, then I shall be
yours." What did she mean by that?

Ramiro addresses Alidoro.

Ah! Mio sapiente venerato Maestro.
Il cor m'ingombra misterioso amore.
Che far degg'io?

Ah! Esteemed and omniscient tutor, my heart
is filled with passion.
What shall I do?

ALIDORO:
Quel che consiglia il core!

ALIDORO:
Do what your heart tells you to do!

RAMIRO:
Principe non sei più: di tante sciocche si vuoti
il mio palazzo!

RAMIRO: *(to Dandini)*
You're no longer to play the role of a prince, so
now get all of those buffoons out of my palace!

(He calls the Courtiers)

Olà, miei fidi. Sia pronto il nostro cocchio, e
fra momenti. Così potessi l'ali dei venti!

Hey, faithful Courtiers, get my carriage ready,
right away. If I only had wings!

Sì, ritrovarla io giuro. Amore, amor mi muove:
se fosse in grembo a Giove, io la ritroverò.

Yes, I vow to find her again. Love spurs me on.
I'll find her even if she is in the arms of Jupiter.

(He gazes at the bracelet)

Pegno adorato e caro che mi lusinghi almeno.
Ah come al labbro e al seno. Come ti stringerò.

This adored and dear token gives me hope. I
will press it to my lips, and to my bosom.

CORO:
Oh! Qual tumulto ha in seno comprenderlo non so!

CHORUS:
What incomprehensible agitation he has in his heart!

RAMIRO e CORO:
Noi voleremo, domanderemo, ricercheremo, ritroveremo.
Dolce speranza, freddo timore dentro al mio/ suo cuore. Stanno a pugnar.
Amore, amore, m'hai/l'hai da guidar.

RAMIRO and CHORUS:
We will hasten, ask, investigate and find her.

The sweetness of hope and cold fear are competing in my/his heart.
Love, guide me! Love, guide him!

Ramiro exits with the Courtiers. Dandini returns.

DANDINI:
Ma dunque io sono un ex? Dal tutto al niente precipito in un tratto?
Veramente ci ho fatto una bella figura!

DANDINI: *(pacing back and forth)*
In one second, I have become an "ex" prince, tumbling from glory to nothing.
But truthfully, I did make a great impression!

Magnifico enters hurriedly.

MAGNIFICO:
Scusi la mia premura. Ma quelle due ragazze stan con la febbre a freddo.
Si potrebbe sollecitar la scelta?

MAGNIFICO: *(to Dandini)*
Excuse my haste, but those two girls are in a cold sweat.
Could you speed up your decision?

DANDINI:
È fatta, amico.

DANDINI:
It's made, my friend.

MAGNIFICO:
È fatta! Ah ! Per pietà! Dite, parlate: è fatta!
E i miei germogli in queste stanze a vegetar verranno?

MAGNIFICO: *(surprised, kneeling)*
It's made! Have mercy and tell me!
Will my two offspring come to flower in these rooms?

DANDINI:
Tutti poi lo sapranno. Per ora è un gran segreto.

DANDINI: *(rising)*
In good time, everyone will know the decision.
But for now, it's a big secret.

MAGNIFICO:
E quale, e quale? Clorinda o Tisbetta?

MAGNIFICO:
Which one? Clorinda or little Tisbe?

DANDINI:
Non giudicate in fretta!

DANDINI:
Don't jump to conclusions!

MAGNIFICO:
Lo dica ad un papà!

MAGNIFICO:
Tell papa your decision!

DANDINI:
Ma silenzio.

DANDINI:
Then don't breathe a word to anyone!

MAGNIFICO:
Si sa; via, dica presto!

MAGNIFICO: *(anxiously)*
Of course! Now, tell me quickly!

DANDINI:
Non ci ode alcuno?

DANDINI: *(looking around)*
Can anyone hear us?

MAGNIFICO:
Non si vede una mosca!

DANDINI:
È un certo arcano che farà sbalordir!

MAGNIFICO:
Sto sulle spine!

DANDINI:
Poniamoci a sedere!

MAGNIFICO:
Presto, per carità!

DANDINI:
Voi sentirete un caso assai bizzarro!

MAGNIFICO:
(Che volesse maritarsi con me!)

DANDINI:
Mi raccomando.

MAGNIFICO:
Ma si lasci servir!

DANDINI:
Sia sigillato quanto ora udrete dalla bocca
mia!

MAGNIFICO:
Io tengo in corpo una segreteria!

DANDINI:
Un segreto d'importanza, un arcano
interessante io vi devo palesar.
È una cosa stravagante,
vi farà trasecolar.

MAGNIFICO:
Senza battere le ciglia. Senza manco trarre il
fiato io mi pongo ad ascoltar. Starò qui
petrificato ogni sillaba a contar.

DANDINI:
(Oh! Che imbroglio! Che disdetta!
Non so come cominciar!)

MAGNIFICO:
(Ve' che flemma maledetta! Si sbrigasse a
incominciar!)

MAGNIFICO:
There's not even a fly on the wall to hear us!

DANDINI:
It's a mystery that will astound you!

MAGNIFICO: *(in a frenzy)*
I'm on pins and needles!

DANDINI: *(bringing a chair)*
Let's sit down!

MAGNIFICO:
For Heaven's sake, hurry up!

DANDINI:
You are about to hear about a fantastic situation!

MAGNIFICO: *(to himself)*
(Maybe he wants to marry me?)

DANDINI:
Please pay attention!

MAGNIFICO: *(with growing impatience)*
At your service!

DANDINI:
You must protect what I now reveal to you:
your lips must be sealed!

MAGNIFICO:
Your secret is safe with me!

DANDINI:
I'm going to reveal a secret of grave importance
to you: a most interesting mystery.
It's an extraordinary situation, and it will
astonish you.

MAGNIFICO:
I'm listening with bated breath, without even
batting an eyelash. I'll sit here in stony silence,
heeding every single syllable.

DANDINI:
(What intrigue! How unfortunate, but I don't
know where to begin!)

MAGNIFICO:
(What cold inhumanity! Hurry up and get
going!)

DANDINI:
Uomo saggio e stagionato sempre meglio ci
consiglia. Se sposassi una sua figlia, come mai
l'ho da trattar?

MAGNIFICO:
(Consiglier son già stampato!)
Ma che eccesso di clemenza! Mi stia dunque
Sua Eccellenza!
(Bestia!) Altezza, ad ascoltar!
Abbia sempre pronti in sala trenta servi in piena
gala, due staffieri, sei cocchieri, tre portieri, due
braccieri, cento sedici cavalli, duchi, conti e
marescialli. A dozzine convitati, pranzi sempre
coi gelati, poi carozze, poi bombè.

DANDINI:
Vi rispondo sensa arcani che noi siamo assai
lontani. Ho un lettino, uno stanzino, ma
piccino, ma meschino.
Io non uso far de' pranzi; mangio sempre degli
avanzi.
Non m'accosto a'gran signori, tratto sempre
servitori.
Ma ne vado sempre a piè, o di dietro una
scappavia, se qualcun mi vuol con sé.

MAGNIFICO:
Non corbella?

DANDINI:
Gliel prometto!

MAGNIFICO:
Questo dunque?

DANDINI:
È una burla il principato, sono un uomo
mascherato.
Ma venuto è il vero Principe m'ha strappata
alfin la maschera.
Io ritorno al mio mestiere: son Dandini il
cameriere. Rifar letti, spazzar abiti far la
barba e pettinar.

MAGNIFICO e DANDINI:
Ah che questa è una sassata che fischiando
inaspettata.
Mi/gli dà in fronte e all'improvviso mi/lo fa in
terra stramazzar.

MAGNIFICO:
Di quest'ingiuria, di quest'affronto il vero
Principe mi renda conto.

DANDINI:
A wise and mature man always possesses the best
advice; if I were to marry one of your daughters,
how do you recommend that I treat you?

MAGNIFICO:
(He's already appointed me Counsellor!)
His graciousness is so excessive!
Your Excellency!
(How Stupid!) Excellency, listen!
At all times, have thirty servants in full livery
ready in the hall, two footmen, six coachmen,
three porters, two laborers, one hundred sixteen
horses, Dukes, Counts, Marshals by the dozens,
meals always with ices, then domed carriages.

DANDINI:
My reply to you is — and I'll make no secret
of it — that your counsel is worthless. I have a
short speech; short, but profound.
I have no use for dinner parties; I always eat
leftovers.
I don't hobnob with fine gentlemen,
and I don't deal with servants.
I always go on foot, or I use a small coach if
someone wants to accompany me.

MAGNIFICO:
Are you joking with me?

DANDINI:
I promise you it's true!

MAGNIFICO: *(looking about)*
But what about all of this luxury?

DANDINI:
It's all a hoax, and this "Prince" business is
nothing but a joke. I am someone else in
disguise; the real prince has returned and
unmasked me.
As such, I am returning to my real job as
Dandini the valet, the man who makes beds,
brushes clothes, shaves beards and dresses hair.

MAGNIFICO and DANDINI:
It's like being unexpectedly hit on the head by
a gigantic boulder/
And my/this head has suddenly fallen to the
ground with a big thud.

MAGNIFICO:
The real prince will owe me an explanation for
this insult and affront.

DANDINI:
Oh non s'incomodi. Non farà niente. Ma parta subito immantinente!

DANDINI:
Don't bother! He will do nothing! Nevertheless, you must leave immediately!

MAGNIFICO:
Non partirò!

MAGNIFICO:
I refuse to leave!

DANDINI:
Lei partirà!

DANDINI:
You <u>will</u> leave!

MAGNIFICO:
Sono un Barone!

MAGNIFICO:
But I am a Baron!

DANDINI:
Pronto è il bastone!

DANDINI:
My stick is ready!

MAGNIFICO:
Ci rivedremo! Ci parleremo!

MAGNIFICO:
We'll see about that! But let's talk about this!

Tengo nel cerebro un contrabasso che basso basso frullando va.
Da cima a fondo, poter del mondo! Che scivolata, che gran cascata!
Eccolo eccolo. Tutti diranno mi burleranno per la città!

I feel like I have a double-bass fiddle whirling deep inside my brains.
By golly, what a disappointment! What a defeat!
The whole town will point their finger at me and mock me!

DANDINI:
Povero diavolo! È un gran sconquasso! Che d'altro in basso piombar lo fa.
Vostr'Eccellenza abbia prudenza. Se vuol rasoio, sapone e pettine saprò arricciarla, sbarbificarla. Ah ah! Guardatelo, l'allocco è là.

DANDINI:
Poor devil! A great embarrassment has made him fall from the heights to the depths. By the way, Your Excellency, be prudent! If you are in need of a razor, soap, or a comb, I can shave you and do your curls. Ha! Ha! Look at this fool!

After Magnifico and Dandini leave, Alidoro appears.

ALIDORO:
Mi seconda il destino. Amor pietoso favorisce il disegno. Anche la notte procellosa ed oscura rende più natural quest'avventura.

ALIDORO:
Just as I planned it, and Cupid approves of my plan. It's a dark and stormy night: the carriage breakdown will seem like a natural accident.

La carozza già è in pronto; ov'è Dandini?
Seco lo vuol nel suo viaggio.
Oh come indocile s'è fatto ed impaziente!
Che lo pizzica amor segno evidente.

The Prince's carriage is ready. Where's Dandini?
The Prince wants him to accompany him. The Prince has become stubborn and impatient, evidence that love tugs at his heartstrings.

Alidoro exits. Cinderella enters, repeating her earlier dream,
"Once upon a time there was a king..."

CENERENTOLA:
Una volta c'era un re, che a star solo s'annoiò:
cerca, cerca, ritrovò, ma il volean sposare in tre.
Cosa fa?

CINDERELLA:
Once upon a time there was a king,
who became bored living without a wife.
He sought and found not one but three suitable brides, all of whom wanted to marry him.
And what did he do?

Sprezza il fasto e la beltà.
E alla fin sceglie per sè l'innocenza e la bontà.
La la là, li li lì, la la là.

He scorned beauty and ostentation, and in the end, chose an innocent and virtuous lady for his bride. La la l, li li li, la la la.

Cinderella stares at her bracelet.

Quanto sei caro! E quello cui dato ho il tuo compagno, è più caro di te. Quel signor Principe che pretendea con quelle smorfie? Oh bella!

How precious you are to me! And the man I gave your companion to, is even more precious. I wonder what the Prince's smirk meant after I renounced material possessions.

Io non bado a'ricami, ed amo solo bel volto e cor sincero, e do la preferenza al suo scudiero. Le miei sorelle intanto, ma che occhiate! Parean stralunate!

The man I love is the Prince's squire: a handsome man with a sincere heart. In the meantime, my stepsisters gave me some real nasty looks! They seemed to be dumbfounded!

A loud knock is heard.

Qual rumore!

Why all that noise?

Cinderella opensthe door, admitting Magnifico and her stepsisters.

(Uh? Chi vedo! Che ceffi!) Di ritorno! Non credea che tornasse avanti giorni!

(Oh? What do I see! What hideous faces!) I didn't expect you to return so soon!

CLORINDA:
(Ma! Ve l'avevo detto!)

CLORINDA: *(to Magnifico)*
(See! It's exactly as I told you!)

MAGNIFICO:
(Ma cospetto! Cospetto! Similissime sono affatto affatto. Quella è l'original, questa è il ritratto.)

MAGNIFICO:
(Good Heavens! They do in fact look very much alike. That other one is the original, and this one the spitting image.)

(to Cinderella, in a rough voice.)

Hai fatto tutto?

Have you done everything I asked you to do?

CENERENTOLA:
Tutto. Perché quel ceffo brutto voi mi fate così?

CINDERELLA:
Yes, everything! Why do you look at me so menacingly?

MAGNIFICO:
Perché, perché, per una certa strega che rassomiglia a te!

MAGNIFICO: *(exasperated)*
Because I have discovered a certain witch who resembles you!

CLORINDA:
Su le tue spalle quasi mi sfogherei!

CLORINDA:
I'd like to vent my malice on your back!

CENERENTOLA:
Povere spalle!
Cosa c'hanno che far?

CINDERELLA:
My poor shoulders!
What do they have to do with it?

Outside, there is thunder and lightning, omens of a threatening storm approaching. The sound of a carriage overturning is head.

TISBE:
O fa mal tempo! Minaccia un temporale.

TISBE:
The weather is bad, and a storm threatens.

MAGNIFICO:
Altro che temporale! Un fulmine vorrei che incenerisse il camerier.

MAGNIFICO:
A storm indeed! I'd like a lightning bolt to strike and incinerate that valet.

CENERENTOLA:
Ma dite? Cosa è accaduto? Avete qualche segreta pena?

CINDERELLA:
Tell me what has happened? Are you in some kind of mysterious trouble?

MAGNIFICO:
Sciocca! Va' là, va' a preparar la cena!

MAGNIFICO: *(vehemently)*
You fool, go and prepare dinner!

CENERENTOLA:
Vado sì, vado! (Ah che cattivo umore. Ah! Lo scudiere mio mi sta nel core!)

CINDERELLA:
Yes, I'm going! (What a bad mood he is in!) Thoughts of my squire occupy my heart!

Dandini enters, followed by Ramiro.

DANDINI:
Scusate, amici. La carrozza del Principe ribaltò.

DANDINI:
Pardon us, friends, but the Prince's carriage has overturned.

Dandini recognizes Don Magnifico.

Ma chi vedo?

Who do I see here?

MAGNIFICO:
Uh! Siete voi! Ma il Principe dov'è?

MAGNIFICO: *(expressing surprise)*
Oh! It's you! But where is the Prince?

DANDINI:
Lo conoscete!

DANDINI: *(pointing to Ramiro)*
Don't you recognize him?

MAGNIFICO:
Lo scudiero? Oh! Guardate!

MAGNIFICO:
Oh, the squire! Oh! Look!

RAMIRO:
Signore perdonate se una combinazione...

RAMIRO:
Sir, forgive me if some circumstance...

MAGNIFICO:
Che dice! Si figuri!
Mio padrone!

MAGNIFICO:
What are you saying?
Don't mention it, my liege!

Magnifico turns to Clorinda and Tisbe.

(Eh non senza perché venuto è qua.
La sposa, figlie mie, fra voi sarà!)
Ehi, presto, Cenerentola, porta la sedia nobile!

(Look, he must have had a reason to come here.
The bride, my daughters, will be one of you!)
Hey, Cinderella, bring our best chair! Quickly!

RAMIRO:
No, no: pochi minuti. Altra carrozza pronta ritornerà.

RAMIRO:
No, I'm only staying a few minutes. Soon, there'll be another carriage coming for me.

MAGNIFICO:
Ma che! Gli pare!

MAGNIFICO:
What do you mean?

CLORINDA:
Ti sbriga, Cenerentola.

CLORINDA: *(rushing toward Cinderella)*
Cinderella, hurry up!

Cinderella returns, carrying an elegant chair for Dandini, who she still believes is the Prince.

CENERENTOLA:
Son qui!

CINDERELLA:
I'm here!

MAGNIFICO:
Dalla al Principe, bestia, eccolo lì!

MAGNIFICO: *(abusively)*
Imbecile, give it to the Prince, over there!

Cinderella suddenly realizes that Ramiro is the real Prince.
She covers her face with her hands and starts to run away.

CENERENTOLA:
Questo! Ah che vedo! Principe!

CINDERELLA:
That man I'm looking at! The Prince!

RAMIRO:
T'arresta! Che! Lo smaniglio! È lei! Che gioia
è questa! Siete voi?

RAMIRO: *(to Cinderella)*
Stay! Oh! The bracelet! It's her! What a great
joy this has become! Is it really you?

CENERENTOLA:
Voi Prence siete?

CINDERELLA: *(observing his clothes)*
Are you really a Prince?

CLORINDA e TISBE:
Qual sorpresa!

CLORINDA and TISBE: *(in amazement)*
What a surprise!

DANDINI:
Il caso è bello!

DANDINI:
What an enchanting series of events!

MAGNIFICO:
Ma...

MAGNIFICO: *(seeking Ramiro's attention)*
But...

RAMIRO:
Tacete!

RAMIRO:
Keep quiet!

MAGNIFICO:
Addio cervello...

MAGNIFICO:
Farewell to my sanity...

DANDINI e RAMIRO:
Silenzio!

DANDINI and RAMIRO:
Let's all quiet down!

TUTTI:
Che sarà! Questo è un nodo avviluppato, questo
è un gruppo rintrecciato.
Chi sviluppa più inviluppa, che più sgruppa,
più raggruppa; ed inanto la mia testa vola, vola
e poi s'arresta; vo tenton per l'aria oscura, e
comincio a delirar.

ALL:
Whatever will be, will be! This is a snarled
knot, with a group of people entangled in it;
the more someone tries to undo it,
the more entangled it becomes. Meanwhile, my
head keeps spinning and stopping. I'm
becoming delirious as I grope about in the dark.

CLORINDA:
Donna sciocca! Alma di fango!
Cosa cerchi? Che pretendi? Fra noi gente
d'alto rango l'arrestarsi è inciviltà.

CLORINDA: *(viciously cursing Cinderella)*
You, stupid woman, with a soul of slime, what
do you want? Who do you think you are? It is
bad manners for you to associate with people
of high breeding like us.

MAGNIFICO:
Serva audace! E chi t'insegna di star qui fra
tanti eroi?
Va' in cucina, serva indegna, non tornar mai
più di qua!

MAGNIFICO:
Who allowed you, audacious servant, to be
presumptuous and associate with such select
company? Go to the kitchen, unworthy servant,
and never again return here!

RAMIRO:
Alme vili! Invan tentate insultar colei che
adoro. Alme vili!
Paventate: il mio fulmine cadrà!

RAMIRO: *(threateningly)*
You despicable people, you insult the one I
adore in vain. Beware, wretched creatures, for
I will strike you in revenge!

DANDINI:
Già sapea che la commedia si cangiava al
second'atto; ecco aperta la tragedia, me la
godo in verità!

DANDINI:
I always knew that this comedy would change
in the second act. The tragedy has now
unfolded, and I'm indeed enjoying it!

CLORINDA e TISBE:
(Son di gelo!)

CLORINDA and TISBE: *(to themselves)*
(I've turned to ice!)

MAGNIFICO:
(So di stucco!)

MAGNIFICO: *(to himself)*
(I'm dumbfounded!)

DANDINI:
(Diventato è un mamalucco!)

DANDINI: *(to himself, about Magnifico)*
(He has transformed into a complete idiot!)

MAGNIFICO, CLORINDA, DANDINI:
Ma una serva!

MAGNIFICO, CLORINDA, DANDINI:
She is but a servant!

RAMIRO:
Olà, tacete! L'ira mia più fren non ha!

RAMIRO: *(threateningly)*
Hey, shut up! I can no longer control my anger.

CENERENTOLA:
Ah! Signor, s'è ver che in petto qualche amor
per me serbate, compatite, perdonate, e
trionfi la bontà!

CINDERELLA: *(gently bowing to Ramiro)*
Lord, if it is really true that you feel love for
me in your heart, pity them and forgive them,
and let goodness be triumphant!

CLORINDA, TISBE, MAGNIFICO:
Ah! L'ipocrita guardate! Oh che bile che mi fa!

CLORINDA, TISBE, MAGNIFICO: *(scornfully)*
That hypocrite! Look at her! She galls me!

DANDINI e RAMIRO:
Quelle lagrime mirate: qual candore, qual
bontà!

DANDINI and RAMIRO:
Look at the sincerity and goodness in those
tears!

MAGNIFICO:
Ma in somma delle somme, Altezza, cosa
vuole?

MAGNIFICO: *(subservient to Ramiro)*
Your Highness, after all is said and done, what
is it that you wish?

RAMIRO:
Piano: non più parole! Questa sarà mia
sposa!

RAMIRO: *(taking Cinderella's hand)*
Quiet! No more discussion! This young lady
will be my bride!

CLORINDA e TISBE:
Ah! Ah! Dirà per ridere!

CLORINDA and TISBE: *(giggling nervously)*
Ha! Ha! He must be joking!

CLORINDA, TISBE, MAGNIFICO:

Non vedi che ti burlano?

RAMIRO:
Lo giuro: mia sarà!

MAGNIFICO:
Ma fra i rampolli miei, mi par che a creder mio...

RAMIRO:
Per loro non son io. Ho l'anima plebea, ho l'aria dozzinale.

DANDINI:
Alfine sul bracciale ecco il pallon tornò e il giocator maestro in aria il ribalzò.

RAMIRO:
Vieni a regnar: lo impongo!

CENERENTOLA:

Su questa mano almeno, e prima a questo seno!

MAGNIFICO:
Ti scosta!

CLORINDA e TISBE:
Ti allontana!

RAMIRO:
Perfida gente insana! Io vi farò tremar!

CENERENTOLA:
Dove son? Che incanto è questo? Io felice! Oh quale evento! È un inganno! Ah! Se mi desto! Che improvviso cangiamento! Sta in tempesta il mio cervello, posso appena respirar!

GLI ALTRI:
Quello brontola e borbotta, questo strepita e s'adira, quello freme, questo fiotta. Chi minaccia, chi sospira: va a finir che a'pazzarelli ci dovranno trascinar.

RAMIRO e DANDINI:
Vieni, vieni. Amor ti guida a regnar e a trionfar!

CLORINDA, TISBE, MAGNIFICO:
(to Cinderella)
Don't you see that they're ridiculing you?

RAMIRO:
I swear that she shall be mine!

MAGNIFICO: *(sheepishly)*
I thought that certainly among my offspring...

RAMIRO: *(contemptuously)*
For them I am not royalty, but rather, a plebeian soul with the bearing of a commoner.

DANDINI:
The Prince is expert and master, righting everything: what goes around comes around.

RAMIRO: *(gently to Cinderella)*
I command you to rule with me!

CINDERELLA: *(turning to kiss Magnifico's hand, and then her stepsisters)*
Allow me to kiss your hand as a sign from my heart!

MAGNIFICO: *(repulsing her)*
Get away from me!

CLORINDA and TISBE:
Go far away!

RAMIRO:
You evil, insane people! I'll make you shudder!

CINDERELLA:
Where am I? Is this sorcery? But at last, I am happy! This is quite an occasion! Could I wake up and find that this is a deceit? Everything has changed so suddenly! My head is spinning and I can hardly breathe!

THE OTHERS:
That one grumbles and mutters, this one shouts and rages. And that one fumes, this one whines, one threatens, another sighs. In the end they'll drag us to the madhouse.

RAMIRO and DANDINI:
Come, let my love guide you to reign in triumph!

Ramiro leaves with Cinderella, followed by Dandini and Magnifico.

TISBE:
Dunque noi siam burlate?

TISBE:
So, we've been duped!

CLORINDA:
Io non vedo più lume!

CLORINDA:
I'm so furious I can hardly see anymore!

TISBE:
Mi pare di sognar; la Cenerentola...

TISBE:
I can't get Cinderella out of mind.

ALIDORO:
Principessa sarà!

ALIDORO: *(entering and interrupting them)*
She shall become a Princess!

CLORINDA:
Chi siete?

CLORINDA:
Who are you?

ALIDORO:
Io vi cercai la carità. Voi mi scacciaste. E
l'Angelina, quella che non fu sorda ai miseri,
che voi teneste come vile ancella, fra la cenere
e i cenci, or salirà sul trono.

ALIDORO: *(haughtily)*
I once asked you for alms, and you both
repulsed me. Cinderella, whom you kept as a
lowly servant amid ashes and rags, will ascend
the throne.

Il padre vostro gli è debitor d'immense somme.
Tutta si mangiò la sua dote. E forse forse questa
reliquia di palazzo, questi non troppo ricchi
mobili, saranno posti al pubblico incanto.

Your father gobbled up her dowry and owes
her enormous sums of money.
Perhaps this old relic of a palace and its ugly
furniture will be sold at public auction.

TISBE:
Che fia di noi, frattanto?

TISBE:
In the meantime, what will happen to us?

ALIDORO:
Il bivio è questo. O terminar fra la miseria i
giorni, o curve a piè del trono implorar grazia
ed impetrar perdono.
Nel vicin atrio io stesso, presago dell'evento,
la festa nuziale ho preparata; questo, questo è
il momento!

ALIDORO:
Either end your days in poverty, or kneel at the
foot of the throne, begging for mercy and
forgiveness. I foresaw this event.
In the hall nearby, they have prepared the
marriage celebration: my great moment of
revenge and celebration!

CLORINDA:
Abassarmi con lei! Son disperata!

CLORINDA:
I despair that I must lower myself to her!

Sventurata! Mi credea comandar seduta in
trono. Son lasciata un'ombra di pietà.

Poor me! I envisioned myself sitting on the throne.
I've lost, and there's not one vestige of pity.

Ma che serve! Tanto fa: sono alfine giovinetta,
capitar potrà il merlotto.
Vo' pelarlo in fretta in fretta e scappar non
mi potrà.
Un marito, crederei, alla fin non mancherà!

But so what! After all, I'm still very young.
When a young man falls into my hands, I'll
quickly pluck his feathers so that he won't run
from me.
But in the end, I will indeed find a husband!

ALIDORO:
La pillola è un po' dura: ma inghiottirla
dovrà; non v'è rimedio.

E voi, cosa pensate?

TISBE:
Cosa penso? Mi accomodo alla sorte. Se mi
umilio, alla fin non vado a morte.

ALIDORO:
The pill is a bit hard to swallow. But there is no
alternative: swallow it she must.

(Alidoro turns to Tisbe.)
And you, what do you think?

TISBE:
What to I think? I accept my fate. I've been
humiliated but it's not the end of my life.

Tosbe expresses her disgust and then exits abruptly.

ALIDORO:
Giusto ciel! Ti ringrazio! I voti miei non han
più che sperar. L'orgoglio è oppresso.
Sarà felice il caro alunno. In trono trionfa la
bontà. Contento io sono!

ALIDORO:
I thank you, merciful Heaven! My wishes have been
totally fulfilled. Excessive pride has been crushed.
My dear pupil shall be happy, and goodness shall
triumph from this throne. I am content!

Alidoro exits.
The final scene is set in an illuminated atrium. Ramiro and Cinderella are seated on
sumptuous thrones, dressed in luxurious finery, while Dandini and Courtiers amble nearby.
Don Magnifico is in a corner, unable to hide his embarrassment.
Alidoro enters, followed by Clorinda and Tisbe,
the latter covering their faces to hide their shame.

CORO:
Della fortuna instabile la revolubil ruota
mentre ne giunge al vertice per te s'arresta
immota. Cadde l'orgoglio in polvere, trionfa la
bontà.

CHORUS: *(to Cinderella and Ramiro)*
The fickle wheel of fortune has reached its
vertex and has stopped for you.
Pride has crumbled to dust and goodness has
triumphed.

RAMIRO:
Sposa!

RAMIRO: *(gently taking Cinderella's arm)*
My bride!

CENERENTOLA:
Signor, perdona. La tenera incertezza che mi
confonde ancor. Poc'anzi, il sai, fra la cenere
immonda. Ed or sul trono, e un serto mi
circonda.

CINDERELLA: *(overwhelmed with joy)*
Lord, forgive my bewilderment and confusion.
As you know, a short while ago I lived amid
the filthy ashes, and now, I have been crowned
and sit on a throne.

MAGNIFICO:
Altezza, a voi si prostra!

MAGNIFICO: *(kneeling before Cinderella)*
Your Highness, I prostrate myself before you!

CENERENTOLA:
Né mai m'udrò chiamar la figlia vostra?

CINDERELLA: *(replying gently)*
Shall I never hear you call me daughter again?

RAMIRO:
Quelle orgogliose!

RAMIRO: *(addressing Cinderella's step-sisters)*
Those arrogant sisters!

CENERENTOLA:
Ah Prence, io cado ai vostri piè.

CINDERELLA:
Prince, I prostrate myself at your feet.

Le antiche ingiurie mi svanir dalla mente. Sul trono io salgo, e voglio starvi maggior del trono, e sarà mia vendetta il lor perdono.

Earlier injustices have vanished from my mind. I rise to the throne, I want to become greater than the throne itself: my revenge shall be to forgive.

Nacqui all'affanno, al pianto. Soffri tacendo il core; ma per soave incanto, dell'età mia nel fiore, come un baleno rapido la sorte mia cangiò.

I was born to sorrow and to misfortune, and my heart suffered in silence. But my fate suddenly changed as joy and happiness overwhelmed me.

Cinderella addresses Magnifico and her stepsisters, who appear moved to tears.

No, no! Tergete il ciglio! Perché tremar, perché? A questo sen volate; figlia, sorella, amica tutto trovate in me.

Dry your tears! Why do you tremble? Come embrace me! In me you will find daughter, sister, and friend.

Cinderella embraces her stepsisters.

TUTTI:
M'intenerisce e m'agita, è un Nume agli occhi miei. Degna del tron tu sei ma è poco un trono a te.

ALL: *(except Cinderella)*
She has stirred and inspired me: in my eyes, she is a goddess. You are worthy of a throne, but a throne is a small reward for you.

CENERENTOLA:
Padre! Sposo! Amico! O instante!

CINDERELLA:
Father! Husband! Friend! What a moment!

Non più mesta accanto al fuoco. Starò sola a gorgheggiar. Ah fu un lampo, un sogno, un gioco il mio lungo palpitar.

I will no longer be alone, sadly singing next to the fire. I became smitten by a dream my heart ached and longed for.

CORO:
Tutto cangia a poco a poco. Cessa alfin di sospirar. Di fortuna fosti il gioco: incomincia a giubilar!

CHORUS:
Everything changes slowly. In time, your sighs will have ceased! Good fortune has entered your life and you can begin to rejoice!

END of OPERA

31994334R00029

Made in the USA
Lexington, KY
02 May 2014